Starmont Reader's Guide
Number Nineteen
ISSN 0272-7730

H. G. WELLS

Robert Crossley

Series Edited by Roger C. Schlobin

BORGO PRESS / WILDSIDE PRESS

www.wildsidepress.com

To My Students at the
University of Massachusetts, Boston

Copyright © 1986 by Starmont House, Inc.
All rights reserved. International copyrights reserved in all countries. No part of this book may be reproduced in any form without the expressed written consent of the publisher.

CONTENTS

Acknowledgments		5
I.	Chronology	7
II.	Wells and Wellsianism: an Assessment	9
III.	*The Time Machine*	20
IV.	*The Island of Dr. Moreau* and *The Invisible Man*	30
V.	*The War of the Worlds* and *The First Men in the Moon*	43
VI.	Short Fiction	58
VII.	Bibliography	67
Index		77

ACKNOWLEDGMENTS

The body of critical writing on H. G. Wells is substantial. It includes so large a measure of original scholarship and attentive interpretation of texts that a commentator lately arriving on the scene may appear ungracious or unaware to offer a book on Wells's science fiction largely innocent of reference to the work of others. I must plead the case for keeping readable a *Guide* designed to be concise and practical. My intellectual debts are documented, at least cursorily, in the secondary bibliography. Readers not familiar with the literary criticism of Wells's fiction are recommended to the studies listed there. Specialists will realize the extent of my debts and will, I trust, excuse the impoliteness of my silences, though of course I seek no excuse for any incorrectness either in my application of the research of my predecessors or in my own reading of Wells. Special acknowledgment must go to the most eminent Wellsians. Bernard Bergonzi, Mark Hillegas, Patrick Parrinder, and Robert Philmus have taught me how to read Wells— and, I hope, how to write about him. The work of W. Warren Wagar has persistently reminded me of the shortsightedness of exclusively literary perspectives on Wells that neglect his value as moralist and ideologue. Since this book was drafted a number of important books on Wells have appeared, notably those by Frank McConnell and John Huntington; the secondary bibliography has been updated to include some of the major work published since 1979.

Whenever possible I quote Wells's texts as they appear in the 1924 Atlantic edition of his works (see item I.B.1 in the primary bibliography). The one exception to this principle is my use of the first edition of *When the Sleeper Wakes*, which I have preferred to the Atlantic edition's printing of the 1910 revision, *The Sleeper Awakes*. For works by Wells published after 1924—not included in any standard collection—I have had to rely on the best texts to which I had access, usually first American editions.

Because the Atlantic edition is available only in research libraries and most readers encounter Wells in paperback reprints, I have not supplied page references. Passages quoted from Wells's novels and novellas are identified by chapter (and, when appropriate, by book and section). Thus a quotation from the fifth chapter of *The Invisible Man* is identified parenthetically as (ch. 5). for *The War of the Worlds* the designation (II, 8) indicates book II, chapter 8. For a more elaborately ordered work like *Men Like Gods* the citation III, 2 : 2) refers to book III, chapter 2, section 2. No effort is made to locate passages quoted from the short stories.

The Time Machine is peculiar in that the first British

edition was divided into 16 chapters followed by an epilogue while other editions used a 12-chapter format with epilogue. Modern paperback reprints vary in chaptering, depending on the editor's choice of copy-text. I will cite both chapterings in the parenthetical reference so that readers may locate the passage no matter which format their own texts adopt. Thus, a reference to *Time Machine* (ch. 2 / 3) indicates that the quoted material appears in chapter 2 of the 12-chapter version and chapter 3 of the 16-chapter version.

My thanks to the University of Massachusetts at Boston for a sabbatical leave during which this book was written and to the English department's colloquium series for a friendly hearing to portions of the first and second chapters. A slightly different version of chapter 3 appeared as "Parables for the Modern Researcher" in *The Malahat Review* (February, 1983). Some of the material in chapter 5 first appeared in *Survey of Science Fiction Literature*, ed. Frank Magill (Salem Press, 1979). To Wendy McGrath and to that enthusiastic utopian Nicky Nickerson, thanks for the typing of the manuscript. My wife, Monica McAlpine, has been characteristically generous with criticism and encouragement and has strengthened this book in many large and small ways which will be known only to us but guessed by those who have benefited from her clear and tactful mind. My most influential muses are named in the dedication; in teaching fantasy and science fiction to them I have felt the urge to write.

I
CHRONOLOGY

1866	born, Bromley, England
1873	breaks leg, begins reading
1879	first literary contacts: Plato, Swift, Johnson, Voltaire, Paine
1881	becomes draper's apprentice
1884	studies biology under Huxley
1888	"Chronic Argonauts" (early version of *Time Machine*)
1891	marries cousin Isabel Wells
1893	turns to journalism
1894	elopes with Amy Catherine Robbins
1895	divorces Isabel; marries Amy Catherine (known as Jane) *The Time Machine*; *The Wonderful Visit*; *The Stolen Bacillus*
1896	*The Island of Dr. Moreau*
1897	*The Invisible Man*; *The Plattner Story*
1898	meets James, Conrad; *The War of the Worlds*
1899	meets Stephen Crane; *When the Sleeper Wakes*; *Tales of Space and Time*
1900	son G. P. ("Gip") born
1901	*First Men in the Moon*
1902	*Anticipations*; *The Sea Lady*
1903	son Frank born; joins Fabians; *Twelve Stories and a Dream*
1904	*The Food of the Gods*

1905	*Modern Utopia; Kipps*
1906	U.S. lecture tour; *In the Days of the Comet*
1908	resigns from Fabians; *The War in the Air*
1909	*Tono-Bungay*
1910	*The Sleeper Awakes* (revision of 1899 edition)
1911	*The Country of the Blind*
1912	takes first airplane ride
1913	begins affair with Rebecca West
1914	son Anthony West born; *The World Set Free*
1915	break with Henry James
1917	advocates League of Nations
1920	visits Lenin; meets Margaret Sanger; *Outline of History*
1921	attends disarmament talks, U.S.
1922	seeks election to Parliament; loses
1923	*Men Like Gods*
1924	start of Atlantic Edition of *Works* (28 vols.)
1927	Jane Wells dies; *Complete Stories*
1933	*The Shape of Things to Come*
1934	meets Stalin, Roosevelt; visits Gorki, Pavlov, Freud; *Experiment*
1936	*Things to Come*
1937	*Star-Begotten*
1940	U.S. lecture tour
1942	Ph.D. thesis in zoology
1945	*Mind at the End of Its Tether*
1946	dies

II
WELLS AND WELLSIANISM: AN ASSESSMENT

A.

More from linguistic custom than with a precise sense of history, we still think of ourselves as in the thick of the Modern Age, though it has now lasted a century or so. H. G. Wells, the author of the most influential works of science fiction in English, was born and grew up during the years in which Darwin and Marx published the fruits of their long researches and speculations and helped provide the intellectual foundations for what is called, by convention, the Modern Age. Later that author would die barely a year after two Japanese cities were subjected to atomic bombardment, thereby inaugurating the Nuclear Age. That age, we know with dreadful certainty, is also ours and we do not know how long it will last. As artist and propagandist, Herbert George Wells was both a celebrator of the intellectual and material promise of the Modern Age and a devout worrier about the human ability to ignore or violate that promise. He spent much of an unusually prolific adult life imagining and espousing the implications of Darwinism, revising and augmenting the utopian possibilities of Marxist socialism, and publicly warning of the danger that the twentieth century might indeed take the road that led to Hiroshima, Nagasaki and beyond.

The speculative fiction on which Wells's literary reputation chiefly rests is motivated by utopian energy and hope and restrained by a Darwinian consciousness of finitude, transience, and the uncertainty of survival. As a Darwinist, Wells believed that the ascendancy of *homo sapiens* on this planet was temporary and provisional. As a utopian socialist, he was dedicated to prolonging and enhancing the human moment on earth; for that task he found Marxism an inflexible and mechanistic instrument, so much attuned to the abolition of an oppressive past that it neglected the creation of a liberating future. In *Men Like Gods*, written in mid-career, he saw Marxism in a state of exhaustion as the Bolshevik revolution was already failing: "The Marxist had wasted the forces of revolution for fifty years; he had had no vision; he had had only a condemnation for established things" (III, 4: 3). Thus the charge Wells later made in his *Experiment in Autobiography*, that Marx was a powerful negative force in modern thought, "an unqualified drag upon the progressive reorganization of human society" (5 : 5). In the last of his full-scale utopias, *The Shape of Things to Come*, he concedes that Marx's theories contained "heroic speculations" which were, nonetheless, diluted by a profound ignorance of history, biology, and "the real psychology of economic activities" (I, 4).

Because he was suspicious of achieved states of perfection, Wells's several utopian narratives endorse an adaptive process of perfectibility—a political condition more akin to Darwinian biology than Marxist economics. Although he appreciated the energy and anarchic splendor of the greatest of the Victorian utopias, William Morris' *News from Nowhere* (1890), he saw its fundamental deficiency as a renunciation of what he called in *A Modern Utopia* "the insubordination of nature" in "this world of conflict" (1 : 1). In fact, Morris' subtitle, *An Epoch of Rest*, must have suggested to Wells exactly the sort of stasis he considered incompatible with modern utopianism. While it is only marginally a work of science fiction, *A Modern Utopia* is, as Wells's first biographer Geoffrey West suggested, "the most characteristic—the most Wellsian—of all his books." Nowhere is it more Wellsian than in its opening paragraph, both a homage to Darwin and a summation of the emphasis on process, choice, adaptability, and evolution central to Wells's vision of the best of human futures:

> The Utopia of a modern dreamer must needs differ in one fundamental aspect from the Nowheres and Utopias men planned before Darwin quickened the thought of the world. Those were all perfect and static States, a balance of happiness won for ever against the forces of unrest and disorder that inhere in things. One beheld a healthy and simple generation enjoying the fruits of the earth in an atmosphere of virtue and happiness, to be followed by other virtuous, happy, and entirely similar generations until the Gods grew weary. Change and development were dammed back by invincible dams for ever. But the Modern Utopia must be not static but kinetic, must shape not as a permanent state but as a hopeful stage leading to a long ascent of stages (1 : 1).

The utopian Wells is a dissenter from the modern literary tradition. While the anti-utopia or "dystopia" is often thought of as a characteristic manifestation of twentieth-century literature, Wells believed, as the title of his greatest utopian document insists, that utopia can be a legitimately modern aspiration. For Wells, utopian speculation was never an idle or self-indulgent pastime. He did not view utopia as simply a wishful alternative to the normal muddle of daily life; it was, rather, the necessary alternative to catastrophe, tyranny, extinction. Human beings had an obligation to work for utopia, to participate in what he called in his later career "an open conspiracy." Otherwise, the gods, grown weary of our inertia, might simply rid themselves of us. While Wells's most famous fictions are exuberant in their display of imagination and invention, many are also grimly cautionary. They serve notice to his post-Darwinian readers that, within certain inflexible cosmic limits, they will choose their future, and that the choice lies between Utopia and Armageddon, between the creation of a new, life-enhancing social order and planetary suicide.

From his first literary success, *The Time Machine*, to his last irritable and disjointed pamphlet, *Mind at the End of Its Tether*, the choice of the future is the issue to which Wells turns and returns most frequently. The nineteenth-century wanderer in the twenty-second century of *When the Sleeper Wakes* states the issue most explicitly: " 'We were making the future,' he said, 'and hardly any of us troubled to think what future we were making'" (ch. 7). In the first great decade of his career, from 1895 to 1905, the issue is explicit in works that describe a hypothetical future (*The Time Machine*, *The Sleeper*) and implicit even in those works not set in the future: the Invisible Man constructs a scenario for the future in which he will prosecute a Reign of Terror; the narrator of *The Island of Dr. Moreau* fears that the events he has witnessed in the Pacific "will be played over again on a larger scale" (ch. 22); the inhabitants of the moon recognize that the coming of the first men to their world prefigures an invasion by the Earth unless they take steps to forestall such a future; the narrator of *The War of the Worlds* cautions his earthly readers that "our views of the human future must be greatly modified" by the experience of extraterrestrial contact (II, 10); and *The Food of the Gods* requires us to "think of all that a harmless-looking discovery in chemistry may lead to" (I, 3 : 5).

After 1905 Wells's pursuit of the issue of making a future became so singleminded, its treatment at times so evangelical, that much of his fiction suffered critical scorn. In fact, apart from a few realistic novels—most of them written before World War I, like *Kipps* and *Tono-Bungay*—from 1905 on, Wells's literary successes were not generally in fiction but in speculative and argumentative prose, in history, autobiography, manifestoes and pamphlets, social prophecy, and political analysis. The utopian Wells persisted, though only seldom in the shape of the romances that characterized his early work.

By the time he reached the age of seventy Wells was so famous that he became passé and the Wellsian doctrine so familiar that readers began to find it tiresome. In his last decade, writing under the shadow and in the heat of a second world war more emphatically global than the first, he grew increasingly fretful and dismayed that his cautions seemed to have gone unheeded. He observed a huge jump in technological sophistication unmatched by a correspondingly wary and disciplined intelligence, so that in his last important work of science fiction, *Star Begotten*, he could lament the peril of a culture in which "the superman makes an aeroplane and the ape gets hold of it" (8 : 2). As the world moved toward the war that would introduce the atomic weapons Wells foresaw in his 1914 novel *The World Set Free*, he seems to have sensed that the choice of a future was being made and that the choice would be Armageddon. The disgusted Professor Keppel in *Star Begotten* may speak for the aging Wells when he realizes he will never hear the music of a saner world: "I am tired of humanity—beyond measure. Take it away. This gaping, stinking, bombing, shooting, throat-slitting, cringing brawl of gawky, under-nourished riff-raff. Clear the earth of them!" (9 : 4). Whether Keppel's voice should be identified with Wells's can be contested, but the epitaph Wells chose for himself in his weary and dispirited last years is brutally unambiguous: "God damn you all. I told you so."

B.

Wells earned the assurance to tell the world off after a long lifetime that began in a dingy, lower middle-class household in the London suburb of Bromley. The son of an unsuccessful shopkeeper and a dutiful housemaid, Wells once traced his intellectual and literary origins to a pair of broken legs. One leg belonged to him at the age of seven and the other, when H. G. was thirteen, to his father Joseph Wells. When he injured his own leg and was invalided, he began to read hungrily anything he could get hold of. Later in life he could remember no titles from this first bout of reading, but the books mattered less than the habit of reading, so adventitiously acquired; that habit kept him from becoming resigned to life as a dry goods clerk—the career his mother kept urging on him.

When Joseph Wells's broken leg ended his part-time work as a cricket player and instructor—income from which supplemented the meager take from his china shop—the family's precarious finances collapsed. Wells's mother Sarah returned to Up Park manor where she had worked before her marriage and resumed duties as a servant. While the experience was humiliating for the Wells family, Joseph Wells's injury gave his son an opportunity to come into contact with a good private library at Up Park. Now some of the books he read *did* matter. In his autobiography he recalls that among the most important were Plato's *Republic*, Johnson's *Rasselas*, the works of Voltaire and Paine, and—a rarity in the Victorian era—an unexpurgated *Gulliver's Travels*. It may be necessary, given Wells's continuing neglect in university curricula, to stress to those Wells once characterized as "pretentious academic greasers" that the author of *The War of the Worlds* and *The Invisible Man* battened on classical and neoclassical literature, on the utopian speculation of Greece, and the satirical and critical minds of the eighteenth-century Enlightenment.

When he was eighteen Wells won a scholarship to the Normal School of Science at South Kensington, a new teacher's college emphasizing technical and vocational training as opposed to the classical humanist curriculum of England's prestigious medieval universities. Wells was lucky enough to encounter one great teacher, the Dean of the School and Professor of Biology, T. H.

Huxley. Although he took only one course with Huxley, for the first time Wells was in the presence of a distinctive mind. In addition to being a spokesman for educational reform (notably in his debate with Matthew Arnold in the 1880's over the places of literature and science in the curriculum), Huxley was also the most famous disciple of Darwin and his most energetic popularizer and defender when Darwinian theory was under attack from conservative Christian apologists. Providing an antidote to the stifling Christianity in which Wells had been reared, Huxley equipped Wells to construct an alternative view of the universe and to ask the questions that generated the fictional masterpieces of the 1890's. Without exaggeration, it can be said that Huxley is the muse Wells most frequently invoked in his early science fiction, especially in *The Time Machine* and *The Island of Dr. Moreau*.

As a student Wells was erratic. He did excellent work when he had inspired instruction. But under the languid and unadventuresome teachers who predominated at the Normal School, Wells cut classes, become a gadfly, acquired informally the rudiments of a political, historical, and literary education, but neglected his formal coursework. He left the school with a mediocre record and got various undistinguished jobs teaching science to preadolescent boys, while trying to steal time to satisfy a sharp desire to write. In the early 1890's, plagued by bad health, unhappily married, and unrewarded—financially or psychologically—by his teaching, Wells risked changing his career to popular journalism. For several years he got by and then his career took a dramatic upward turn in 1895 with the publication of *The Time Machine*, which he had been composing and revising over seven years. Its commercial and critical success was sufficient to give Wells a secure basis on which to build the massive body of writing of his next fifty-one years.

The science fiction, which remains the enduring artistic product of Wells's career, is concentrated mostly in the first ten years; his most famous longer works and nearly all his short stories were in print by 1905. A few significant works of science fiction—including *In the Days of the Comet*, *The War in the Air*, *Men Like Gods*, *The Shape of Things to Come*, and *Star Begotten*—were written after that remarkable decade, however, and are reminders that science fiction remained a useful literary form for Wells even after his priorities as a writer changed. While all the undisputed masterpieces of speculative fiction were published early, his later career is brilliant in other respects. He moved from pure fantasy to applied fantasy, from the literature of awe to the rhetoric of persuasion. Only the narrowest academic or aesthetic bias will see such a movement as necessarily a decline in power, intelligence, or significance. Wells's propagandizing later years are, in central ways, the natural outcome, the fruit of his early years of artful experiment and triumph. The scope of this *Guide* necessarily does a disservice to one of Wells's masterpieces, *A Modern Utopia*, and to such underestimated later romances as *The War in the Air* and *Star*

Begotten. The truth is that Wells the utopian propagandist is closer to the essential Wells of the early speculative romances than is usually admitted. Still, for the purposes of a brief *literary* guide, the first ten years must take precedence. But it is important to keep in mind that for Wells the fiction of 1895-1905 for which he is remembered was the beginning—not the culmination—of his mature work.

C.

Wells did not write what is now know, modishly, as SF. Still less did he write what is called, disparagingly, "sci-fi." He did not even name his early works "science fiction." That term came into use later in the twentieth century, under American auspices, out of the pulp magazines of the twenties and thirties. The term "science fiction" has now become so inclusive and heterogeneous a designation of literary form, a label so inexact and makeshift that nearly any generalization about it is likely to be rash or inane. And yet to read what Wells called his "scientific romances" is to be convinced that generalization about his role in shaping modern science fiction is an obligation of honesty, at least. There is such a thing as a Wellsian tradition in science fiction—the only line of development in the genre that can be identified by the name of a single author. There are still some fussy readers and writers of science fiction who insist on distinguishing science fiction from so-called "mainstream" literature. But within the capacious genre of science fiction, the Wellsian tradition can claim to *be* the mainstream.

Wells is not the father of modern speculative romance. Science fiction's parent is Mary Shelley, whose *Frankenstein* (1818) mischievously but firmly corrects the inclination to assign only fathers to acts of creation. If one insists on locating a father for science fiction, that distinction goes to Jules Verne—a distinction, it should be stated, of considerably less value than Wells's. The emphasis is needed because, after all this time, Wells and Verne still are often linked in the popular mind. But Verne wrote books for adolescent boys and pedants. Books about gadgets and exotic locales. Books of popular science leavened with a modicum of adventure, episodic books with little thematic unity and less intellectual substructure. Many of Verne's romances have been accurately reproduced on film by Walt Disney's studios. While not particularly interesting films for adults, they are fair reflections of the spirit of their originals. Wells's romances have also tempted directors, but the results have rarely been satisfying. The major exceptions are James Whale's splendid 1932 version of *The Invisible Man* (which Wells in his autobiography claimed to enjoy) and the two cinematic adaptations of his work in which Wells had a hand. The better known of the two is *Things to Come* (1936), directed by William Cameron Menzies from Wells's screenplay. Although dated in some respects and hampered by frequently wooden acting, *Things to Come* retains considerable visual power and remains one of the few interesting (if not wholly convincing) filmed utopias. Less often seen is *The Man Who Could Work Miracles* (1935), a witty and lively rendition of Wells's 1898 short story of the same name, for which the author again supplied a screenplay.

The disappointing quality of most of the visual adaptations is a reminder of how much Wells's science fiction depends for its success on its verbal energy. When his fiction works it is affecting because of, not despite, its use of language. Such a statement may seem grossly self-evident, except that science fiction has so often been defended by partisans (and reviled by those who refuse to read it) as a literature of pure ideas and cheap thrills, unburdened by a concern for the graceful, fresh, or even precise use of words. Wells's most accomplished fictions merit no such defense or condescension. Even some of his flawed or careless books, notably *When the Sleeper Wakes* and *The Food of the Gods*, are rich and provocative enough to have generated books by other writers that surpassed their models. Wells taught a great many other people how to write science fiction. In fact, Wells has become part of the mythology *within* science fiction. In *Out of the Silent Planet* (1938) C. S. Lewis' Ransom anticipates his experiences on Mars by reminding himself, "He had read his H. G. Wells." The time-traveling protagonist in Michael Moorcock's *The Warlord of the Air* (1971) is needled by a skeptical military man: "Probably been reading a bit too much H. G. Wells, eh?" Even Wells himself, in his final work of science fiction *Star Begotten* (1937), alludes mischievously to one of his first romances when the characters discuss the possibility of an extraterrestrial invasion: "Some of you may have read a book called *The War of the Worlds*—I forget who wrote it—Jules Verne, Conan Doyle, one of those fellows" (2:3). As Wells knew perfectly well, people were not likely to forget who created the modern myth of an invasion from Mars. In Saul Bellow's *Mr. Sammler's Planet* (1970) the homage to Wells is a continuing motif and the protagonist's daughter observes at one point, "She had H. G. Wells on the brain, the large formation of a lifetime. H. G. Wells was the most august human being she knew of." An industrious researcher who itemized the number of *fictional* characters who have "been reading a bit too much H. G. Wells" might discover just how deeply Wellsianism has infiltrated the consciousness of modern writers. Could it be that there is some of the artist's pride in his progeny as well as a forsaken prophet's desolation in "God damn you all. I told you so"?

Some writers who have followed Wells, who make up the Wellsian tradition, have superseded him in particular ways. Olaf Stapledon is a deeper and more original thinker. C. S. Lewis, alternately fascinated and troubled by Wells, has a greater gift for wedding the visual to the speculative. Yevgeny Zamyatin's *We*, arguably the most moving of twentieth-century dystopias, is at once a tribute to Wells and a brilliant upstaging of *When the Sleeper Wakes*. Ursula Le Guin produces fictions as generous in scope and as committed to utopian principle as Wells's, but with a sureness of characterization he never mastered. Arthur C. Clarke's *Childhood's End* presents an evolutionary breakthrough to *homo superior*—a mythic narrative more conducive to awe and applause than Wells's more muddled efforts in *The Food of the Gods* and *In the Days of the Comet*. John Brunner and J. G. Ballard employ a Wellsian imagination of disaster in anticipating the near future, but both are technical innovators whereas Wells rarely strayed from sequential narrative. And so on. Examples could be multiplied, but the point is simple. A Wellsian tradition exists, and while many of Wells's descendants have enhanced and refined features of the work he originated, none supplants him. He is the one irreplaceable figure in the history of science fiction.

If Wells isn't the father of modern science fiction, then he is that more formidable figure, its godfather. The old man who created a literary dynasty, whom people as various as Aldous Huxley and George Orwell, Hilaire Belloc and C. S. Lewis have attempted to kill off by polemic and parody, whom academics have tried to suffocate by excluding his works from the classroom and literary histories, whom every major writer of speculative romance must acknowledge by imitation, extension, or repudiation. Wells cannot be evaded. He survives. He is big. His impact on the development of modern fiction (the term "science fiction" will soon be both an archaism and a redundancy) is so massive that it beggars description in a couple of paragraphs.

D.

Most of Wells's aims as an imaginative writer can be glossed with an episode from *When the Sleeper Wakes*. When the protagonist, a nineteenth-century man named Graham who awakes in the twenty-second century, asks the dictator Ostrog to explain the situation of the common man in the future society, Ostrog urges him to read "our realistic novelists." Graham's reply amounts to Wells's creed: "I want reality, not realism" (ch. 19). The reality Wells wanted to exhibit in his science fiction was mysterious, sometimes exhilarating, often forbidding, more formidable and enduring than human life, intractable. Realism, as practiced by Wells's one-time friend and eventual antagonist Henry James, demanded a clean, well-lighted universe, an intricate structure—made perhaps by God but ordained, surely, for man—over which human intelligence and art could preside with comfortable assurance. Wells, raised on Plato, Swift, and Johnson, was always in profounder sympathy with the Johnsonian injunction to "regulate imagination by reality" than with the Jamesian notion of building a "house of fiction."

Wells's distaste for the aesthetic of Jamesian realism has often been taken as a confession of artlessness. In fact, as he grew older and more isolated from the literary community, Wells did stiffen his back and encourage classification of himself as a journalist rather than an artist. From the time of his falling-out with Henry James in 1915, Wells cherished the role of iconoclast, the icons being the emerging practitioners of the "modern" novel. "I am," he once asserted with evident vanity, "the absolute antithesis of Mr. James Joyce." But Wells's polemical characterization of his hostility to art is not a dispassionate appraisal of his work; it is an aggressive posture of self-defense more revealing of Wells the man than of the integrity of his fiction.

Some Wellsian narrators, particularly in the early short stories, may seem to support the view of Wells as journalist rather than artist. The narrator of "The Plattner Story" is a representative example:

> I have resisted, I believe successfully, the natural disposition of a writer of fiction to dress up incidents of this sort. I have told the thing as far as possible in the order in which Plattner told it to me. I have carefully avoided any attempt at style, effect, or construction.

But the import of this passage—apart from its portrait of a type of rational, skeptical, plain-spoken mind that often served Wells's purpose as a conduit of irrational and disturbing events—is to propound an antidecorative aesthetic. It announces that Wells will not write science fiction as Poe might have written it or display the paranormal as James displays it in "The Turn of the Screw." Wells's fiction has a distinctive style that grows out of his determination to seek and present the reality lodged within fantastic occurrences. Long before Norman Mailer and Truman Capote, Wells was exploring the aesthetic possibilities of fusing fiction and journalistic convention into a style at once both fantastic and matter-of-fact.

The famous opening paragraph of *The War of the Worlds* is the definitive instance of fictional reportage, of the documentary imagination in Wells's fiction. He does not abjure style, effect, or design, but he seeks appropriate strategies of narration for improbable events—in this case, a post-catastrophic reconstruction of a war between Earth and Mars. With its declarative, cumulative weight, the paragraph steadily drives a wedge between reality, things as they are, and man's "realistic" conception of human hegemony. What only recently was thought incredible is now universally acknowledged as real:

> No one would have believed in the last years of the nineteenth century that this world was being watched keenly and closely by intelligences greater than man's and yet as mortal as his own; that as men busied themselves about their various concerns they were scrutinised and studied, perhaps almost as narrowly as a man with a microscope might scrutinise the transient crea-

tures that swarm and multiply in a drop of water. With infinite complacency men went to and fro over this globe about their little affairs, serene in their assurance of their empire over matter. It is possible that the infusoria under the microscope do the same. No one gave a thought to the older worlds of space as sources of human danger, or thought of them only to dismiss the idea of life upon them as impossible or improbable. It is curious to recall some of the mental habits of those departed days. At most, terrestrial men fancied there might be other men upon Mars, perhaps inferior to themselves and ready to welcome a missionary enterprise. Yet across the gulf of space, minds that are to our minds as ours are to those of the beasts that perish, intellects vast and cool and unsympathetic, regarded this earth with envious eyes, and slowly and surely drew their plans against us. And early in the twentieth century came the great disillusionment (I, 1).

The paragraph is carefully orchestrated to build toward the elaborate proportional measurement of Martian, human, and animal minds and to yield up the "disillusionment" of the closing periodic sentence. Like the microscopic bacteria and the beasts that perish, human dignity and durability appear ephemeral when measured against a larger scale. Scrutinized and studied by envious Martian eyes, humanity becomes a zoological specimen, a bit of the solar system's wildlife whose habitat might be appropriated for other uses. Although the human species survives the war of the worlds, its pride is chastened. Stripped of the fancies and mental habits of regarding itself as unique, alone, specially favored by God, *homo sapiens* must surrender its imperial conceits.

The beginning of *The War of the Worlds* is more than a stylistic *tour de force*; it is at the center of the moral vision that underlies and invigorates Wellsian fiction. In the preface to a 1934 reissue of his early scientific romances, Wells described them as "consciously grim, under the influence of Swift's tradition" and as an "assault on human self-satisfaction." *The War of the Worlds* may be his most relentlessly Swiftian castigation of sentimental humanism. The disenchantment of *homo sapiens*, as Wells must have seen it, was long overdue. Even after the Copernican revolution upset the geocentric universe and proposed that the Earth was but one satellite of one star, human beings clung to the comforting myth of a *homo*centric universe: though our planet is off-center, we are yet the crown of creation, the reason for the creation's being. Darwin and Huxley, furnishing the biological arguments to complement the astronomical evidence of man's tangential place in the scheme of things, had been unable to dislodge the old illusions. Only an invasion could accomplish that. And so Wells imagined one. *The War of the Worlds* is his impassive obituary on homocentric fantasies and the literature and philosophy which support them.

"The great disillusionment" is the distinctive characteristic of Wellsianism. It is not a motif limited to those earliest of Wells's fictions that are so uncompromising in their spectacles of human fragility and disaster, for disillusionment is not merely or necessarily an invitation to indulge feelings of despair or futility. The stripping away of illusion and particularly of disabling self-delusion can be the sign of the recovery of spiritual health, of the self-knowledge that is wisdom's beginning, of the dismantling that is the necessary prelude to the construction of an unsentimental utopia.

Contrary to some critical truisms, Wells is neither a man of irreconcilable "optimistic" and "pessimistic" phases nor a writer unable to decide between the claims of art and ideology. He is the great disillusioner for the post-Copernican, post-Darwinian, post-Christian, post-humanist world who offers his readers the bracing dose of reality and the liberated imagination necessary for building and inhabiting a viable future. From first to last in his important works of science fiction, Wells insists on the necessity of shedding illusions—and the rigidity of mind and habit attendant on them—to acquire the versatility, adaptability, and imagination we need to reinvent ourselves and our world. As the still unexcelled genius of speculative romance, he chose forms of fiction most identified with illusion, fantasy, dreams, and imaginary worlds as the instruments for cleansing the diseased fantasies, upsetting the mental and moral inertia, loosening the dangerous certitudes of modern readers. H. G. Wells is among the least escapist writers of the twentieth century.

III
THE TIME MACHINE

The distinctive place of *The Time Machine* in modern literature is the result of Wells's decision not simply to depict a future but to construe future history. The voyage through time belongs to the stock in trade of satiric fantasy, an updated version of the familiar oceanic travelogue of a restless Sindbad or naive Gulliver. But the boldness of Wells's design lies in his effort to speculate how human society, or its vestiges, in the far future would be dependent on, derived from, historically linked to human society in 1895. Further, Wells did not limit himself to political or sociological future history; he took pains to produce an authentic forecast of the planetary as well as the human condition. In the climactic episode called "The Further Vision," which leaps forward 30,000 millennia beyond the reign of Queen Victoria, he sketches the world's end with all the symbolic resonance of scriptural eschatology and the data of scientific observation—and the terror of both.

Conceptually and formally *The Time Machine* has set a standard for much subsequent science fiction. And yet, for all its novelty and artfulness, Wells's romance is not something altogether new under the sun. *The Time Machine* has the originality of a hybrid. Imagining alternative forms of human society is the chief motive of utopian fiction, a polemical literary form that had been flourishing for at least 2400 years, from Plato onwards. And the creation of fictive history is perhaps a more ancient and persistent imaginative endeavor, reaching back to the legendary history enshrined in Homer's epics and stretching forward to the post-Gibbonian historical novel of the nineteenth century. By joining utopian romance to historical fiction Wells gave *The Time Machine* the vigor that is often missing when genres keep producing inbred progeny. Rooting his alternative society in a rigorous, though selective, extrapolation from his own present, Wells derived a more cheerless view of future humanity than was common in utopian fiction. At the same time his insistence on looking to and confronting the future we are making kept him from falling into the paralyzing nostalgia that is the great temptation of the historical novel. A journey to the future is not necessarily an escape from the here and now; it may in fact be harder to evade present troubles by traveling to the future than by rehearsing the past. Matthew Arnold's essay "Literature and Science" (1882)—part of his famous debate with Wells's mentor, T. H. Huxley—promotes a far more escapist attitude to the literature of the past than anything a reader will find in Wells's romances of the future.

It is worth remembering that the time machine is *capable* of sending the traveler backwards as well as forwards in time—a potentiality stressed at the opening of the narrative and in the epilogue. Why then does Wells's protagonist push only the forward lever? As his novella "A Story of the Stone Age" demonstrates, Wells was not uninterested in the past and in what we might learn about ourselves as civilized creatures through a fictive reconstruction of the psychology of paleolithic man. But the time traveler goes to the future because that is the only direction a time machine is really good for—unless one wants to be nothing more than a sightseer or meddler in history. There are fossils, artifacts, and documents that provide avenues into past history; but one has to invent a way to cut a path into future history. Wells's machine is the imaginative equivalent of the archeologist's pickaxe and the historian's card catalogue. It is a tool of "presearch."

Conceptually, the time machine and its forward motion are not arbitrary devices but basic to the intellectual design of the narrative. Practically, the machine is another matter. As Wells presents it, it is a gleaming, ungainly piece of gimmickry. We are never given an engineer's description, only a cunningly impressionistic glimpse of metal, ivory, and crystal in a shadowy room lit by a flickering candle. In the preface to a 1934 reissue of his early romances, Wells made no bones about the sleight-of-hand underlying his speculative fiction: "For the writer of fantastic stories to help the reader play the game properly, he must help him in every possible unobtrusive way to *domesticate* the impossible hypothesis. He must trick him into an unwary concession to some plausible assumption and get on with his story while the illusion holds." In the first chapters of *The Time Machine*, the verbal flim-flam of the traveler's lecture on the theory of time and the mechanics of his invention is designed to get us to concede the premise of the central narrative. The idea of time travel may seem plausible if we are hurried through it and hurried past the marvelous tinkertoy sitting in the lab. Measured against the more sophisticated treatments of the mechanics, psychology, ethics, and aesthetics of time travel in later works of science fiction like C. S. Lewis' *The Dark Tower*, Stanislaw Lem's *Star Diaries*, Octavia Butler's *Kindred*, and Marge Piercy's *Woman on the Edge of Time*, Wells's illusion here is flimsy and his machine quaint.

But Wells was interested chiefly in a pretext for the adventures in ideas which make up the bulk of *The Time Machine*. Though his aim is speculation, his mode is romance. And that mode is evident not just in the strategy of domesticating the impossible but in the very setting for the traveler's narration—a setting that links Wells's to such other romances as the voyages of Sindbad from *The Thousand and One Nights*. Like Sindbad, the time traveler returns from his voyages to a gathering of friends and acquaintances, feasts them, and offers as an after-dinner speech an autobiographical travelogue. For all its sober exploration of future history, of human degeneration and planetary death, *The Time Machine* belongs to the leisurely atmosphere of the dinner hour when, as the narrator says, "thought runs gracefully free of the trammels of precision" (ch. 1). The circumstantial details of dinner parties in mundane Victorian England root the romance of time travel in a solid, if somewhat genially caricatured, reality. At the same time, because the tale is not told in a lecture hall or on a witness stand but over brandy and cigars with the traveler's explicit proviso that he will not entertain interruptions or objections, the narration is exempted from verification and is granted the usual privileges of romance.

The traveler begins brilliantly with an extended sensory montage of his ride into the future, so exciting and convincing an account of what it might feel like to time-travel that whatever lingering disbelief remains in the machine itself is gladly suspended. As the traveler accelerates, description becomes vision and the landscape acquires something of the living radiance Wordsworth sees during his ascent of Mount Snowdon in the last book of *The Prelude*: [1]

> The dim suggestion of the laboratory seemed presently to fall away from me, and I saw the sun hopping swiftly across the sky, leaping it every minute, and every minute marking a day....The twinkling succession of darkness and light was excessively painful to the eye. Then, in the intermittent darknesses, I saw the moon spinning swiftly through her quarters from new to full, and had a faint glimpse of the circling stars. Presently, as I went on, still gaining velocity, the palpitation of night and day merged into one continuous greyness; the sky took on a wonderful deepness of blue, a splendid luminous colour like that of early twilight; the jerking sun became a streak of fire, a brilliant arch, in space; the moon a fainter fluctuating band....
> ...I saw trees growing and changing like puffs of vapour, now brown, now green; they grew, spread, shivered, and passed away. I saw huge buildings rise up faint and fair, and pass like dreams. The whole surface of earth seemed changed—melting and flowing under my eyes (ch. 3/4).

This is the romancing Wells at his best; language and idea, speculation and sensation are seamless. The vision of a kinetic, liquefied world is an image of change Wells returned to frequently in his science fiction to suggest both a wondrous metamorphosis—as here and in the account of the "slushy liquefaction" of the lunar atmosphere at sunrise in *The First Men in the Moon* (ch. 6)—and more often, the destruction and dissolution of human culture. During the panic of exodus from London, urban institutions "were losing coherency, losing shape and efficiency, guttering, softening, running at last in that swift liquefaction of the social body" (*The War of the Worlds*, I, 16). The most sustained description of the effects of atomic war in *The World Set Free* is the flooding of the Netherlands when the warheads destroy the dikes (2 : 7-9). In *The War in the Air*, the bombs falling on the world's cities are described as themselves molten: "The war comes through the air, bombs drop in the night. Quiet people go out in the morning, and see air-fleets passing overhead—dripping death—dripping death!" (7 : 7). Even in the very late *Star-Begotten*, the metaphor survives, though more abstractly: "Our world is in liquidation" (10 : 1).

In *The Time Machine* the traveler arrives in the future "wet to the skin," trailing his clouds of glory in the form of a thundering hailstorm, a meteorological disturbance caused, presumably, by his machine's sudden eruption into the future landscape and atmosphere. The temporal odometer on the machine reads 802,701. Since he voyages only in time, not in space, the traveler remains in what used to be a London suburb. But finding himself in a semitropical garden, he is inclined to judge this future as a new golden age, Eden restored, an achieved utopia. The inhabitants he first encounters are pretty, youthful, laughing, dressed in short, flowing robes, bare-legged and bare-headed, hairless except for uniformly curly coiffures, speaking in a "very sweet and liquid tongue," four feet tall, thin, androgynous, and vegetarian (ch. 3-4/4-5). They are the personification of innocence, of freedom from drudgery and pain, of harmony with their natural environment. Or so the traveler wants to believe. But one of the crucial lessons of his travels is the limits of deduction in an alien world. His speculation about the future locates the truth only after a long and blundering series of revised interpretations.

Despite his desire to find the image of utopia in the future, from the very beginning the traveler sees things that puzzle him and make him apprehensive. A leprous white sphinx broods over the lawn where his machine rests. An emblem of the riddle of the future that perplexes the traveler, the statue colors the entire narrative with suggestions of disease and dying. The garden itself is tangled and untended. Nearby are massive buildings badly in need of repair. Inspecting the neighborhood, the traveler finds tumbled heaps of granite, marble, and aluminum. He is served fruits resembling "hypertrophied" raspberries and oranges. His diminutive hosts, whom he learns to call Eloi, seem less like children than a race in its second childhood—slow, addled, unresourceful, and, as events unfold, vulnerable and resigned. Their mellifluous language is barely capable of predication. In the evening they nestle together like kittens in the ruined palaces. The more he looks, the more the traveler sees a world overripe and debilitated, the human community shrunken and attenuated.

The human species, the traveler supposes, has civilized itself flat out of its humanity. In triumphing over nature, the species has eliminated energy, initiative, and independence along with disease and inconvenience. Without necessity to keep their wits sharp, their muscles toned, and their imaginations alive, the Eloi fall victim to their own security and slip into langour, decadence, and quietude. But this initial Darwinian interpretation is incomplete, only "a glimpse of one facet of the truth" (ch. 4/6), as the traveler comes to realize. There is other evidence he needs if he is going to construe the history of the future accurately.

Only after discovering that his machine has been stolen and that the Eloi are too weak and witless for theft does the traveler suspect that there is other intelligent—or at least resourceful—life in 802,701. While searching for the machine, he catches sight of a whitish animal, resembling a small deer, slipping through the underbrush at twilight. That creature—described in a profusion of animal and insect metaphors throughout the narrative—is a Morlock. Stoop-shouldered, with large eyes sensitive to sunlight, covered thickly on head and back with yellowish hair, the Morlocks are the other humanoid species of the future. They are, as it were, the invisible men of the 8028th century—out of sight and, by daylight at least, out of the Eloi's mind. It takes time for the traveler to put the evidence together: the cupolas and wells dotting the landscape, the absence of cemeteries among the Eloi, the taboos on discussion of the Morlocks, the identity and location of the textile workers who furnish the Eloi their fine clothing. But even before the traveler grasps the Morlocks' role in the food chain and in the remnants of human culture, he feels a visceral revulsion, "a peculiar shrinking from those pallid bodies" (ch. 6/9). What they are he cannot tell, but the traveler knows he hates them.

Throughout his voyage the traveler's judgment is often hostage to desire and prejudice. He is never entirely the detached observer of the future, but he falls incessantly into the habits of assessment characteristic of his social class and Victorian culture. Although neither Morlocks nor Eloi are properly human but only humanoid, the traveler finds his sympathies bent to the Eloi. While exploring one of the Morlock caverns, he stumbles into a vast dining room dominated by a joint of red meat. He is too slow to perceive at once that the meat is protein-rich Eloi-flesh, but the sight gives him what he thinks of as an *instinctive* loathing of the Morlocks. When he flees their tunnel he gets a close-up view of their faces, as he tells his captive after-dinner audience with whom he has been appeasing his own craving to "stick a fork into meat again" and "get some peptone into my arteries" (ch. 2/3). "You can scarce imagine," he says, "how nauseatingly inhuman they looked—those pale, chinless faces and great, lidless, pinkish-grey eyes!—as they stared in their blindness and bewilderment. But I did not stay to look, I promise you" (ch. 6/9). Just so might a squeamish Victorian gentleman have shuddered, averted his eyes, and retreated from an East End London slum. The traveler's "instincts" are, in fact, the politically conditioned reflexes of his own proper era. Later, reflecting on his horror of the Morlocks, he recognizes them as the heirs of the urban poor of the nineteenth century, no longer submissive and resigned to their fate:

> Ages ago, thousands of generations ago, man had thrust his brother man out of the ease and sunshine. And now that brother was coming back—changed! Already the Eloi had begun to learn one old lesson anew. They were becoming reacquainted with Fear. And suddenly there came into my head the memory of the meat I had seen in the Underworld (ch. 7/10).

The traveler's political analysis is never thoroughly successful. At various times he tries to rise above the biases of his class and repress his "instinctual" aversions by seeking impersonal anthropological, moral, and historical explanations for the Morlocks' atavistic cannibalism and the bovine passivity of the Eloi. But all these postures of detachment fall because finally, in the traveler's jaded eyes, the Eloi *look* more human than the Morlocks. The notion that effete, angular, skinny, hairless, leisured, thoughtless wastrels are more essentially or profoundly human than hirsute, appetitive, stooped, sneaky mechanics and laborers should not be mistaken for a dispassionate evaluation. When the traveler claims that the Eloi "had kept too much of the human form not to claim my sympathy" (ch. 7/10), we should recall the truncated experience of the Victorian gentleman that biases his eye and corrupts his judgment.

The outstanding instance of the traveler's acculturated biases is his relationship to Weena, the member of the Eloi he rescues from drowning early in his stay. The androgyny of the Eloi makes it hard to distinguish them sexually and the traveler first refers to Weena as "my little woman, as I believe it was" (ch. 5/8). Initially he sees Weena as alien and neuter, an "it," but thenceforth he *chooses* to use the feminine pronoun. This is not an objective assignment of gender; the traveler simply sees what he desires to find—a "little woman" by his side. Lonely and homesick, he adopts a quasi-spousal, if not exactly sexual, attachment to Weena. The language of his description emphasizes the comfort Weena gives him, though it is the ineffectual comfort of the stereotypical troublesome helpmate. She becomes a bachelor's fantasy of connubial security and devotion, a "little doll of a creature" whose clinging loyalty gives the traveler "almost the feeling of coming home" (ch. 5/8). The traveler humanizes this fantastic alien as a man humanizes his dog by turning dumb fidelity into a facsimile of love. In a moment of partial lucidity on this subject, the traveler indicates his awareness that he is interpreting Weena to fit his desires: "She always seemed to me, I fancy, more human than she was, perhaps because her affection was so human" (ch. 8/11). [2].

Eventually Weena becomes, as well, the traveler's trophy, the booty from his venture to the future which he must keep secure from the predatory Morlocks. "Weena I had resolved to bring with me to our own time" (ch. 7/10) he comments on his expedition to the Palace of Green Porcelain, a derelict museum where he procures weapons—inflammable camphor and an iron lever to be wielded as a mace—for use against the Morlocks. The traveler gives no thought to how Weena would survive in the alien world of 1895; his action is not rational but fanciful and proprietary. His conception of Weena is partly chivalric, partly troglodytic. Weena becomes his lady and the museum their castle as the traveler, "mace in one hand and Weena in the other," stalks through the galleries searching for Morlock skulls to smash (ch. 8/11); it is a scene that might have been enacted by Ugh-lomi and Eudena, Wells's paleolithic hero and heroine of the year 50,000 B.C. in "A Story of the Stone Age." Wells's other time traveler, Graham in *When the Sleeper Wakes*, directly acknowledges his primitivism in the nearer future of the twenty-second century: "I am uncivilised. I am primitive—Palaeolithic" (ch. 20). The resurgence of primitive impulse occurs more gradually and dramatically in *The Time Machine* as the traveler slowly descends into barbarism, becoming an illustration of devolution, rather than evolution, of the brutishness of survival that characterizes both man's pre-civilized past and his post-civilized future.

That development is clearest in the final flight through the woods. As fire fails the traveler, he and Weena become prey to the soft, searching fingers of the hungry Morlocks, and the nineteenth-century man sheds the last vestiges of bourgeois gentility:

> I was caught by the neck, by the hair, by the arms, and pulled down. It was indescribably horrible in the darkness to feel all these soft creatures heaped upon me. I felt as if I was in a monstrous spider's web. I was overpowered, and went down. I felt little teeth nipping at my neck. I rolled over, and as I did so my hand came against my iron lever. It gave me strength. I struggled up, shaking the human rats from me, and holding the bar short, I thrust where I judged their faces might be. I could feel the succulent giving of flesh and bone under my blows, and for a moment I was free.
>
> The strange exultation that so often seems to accompany hard fighting came upon me. I knew that both I and Weena were lost, but I determined to make the Morlocks pay for their meat. I stood with my back to a tree, swinging the iron bar before me (ch. 9/12).

Here is Darwinian man at work—and at play. It is as if the protagonist recapitulates the psychological and sexual exhilaration that may have animated the first paleolithic ancestor of man who put hand to club and discovered power. In recovering his primitive self the traveler makes clear to us, even if he himself evades it, that however much his physical form may seem to him to link him to the Eloi, in temper and spirit and blood he is profoundly Morlockian.

Only when Weena is lost is the spell broken for the traveler. He is briefly tempted to a final outburst of bloodlust when he allows his imagination to picture Weena's body lying on the Morlocks' supper table. But the chief effect of Weena's loss is the attainment of a more balanced perspective. Weena gone, the traveler can see the Morlocks, wandering and choking through the forest fired by his camphor, as pitiable, as "damned souls"—though, in his immediate crisis, they remain the enemy.

Just before the traveler recovers his machine and escapes into time, we are given our last prospect view of the world 800,000 years from now. Climbing a low hill, the traveler scans the Thames valley and sees not the paradise or utopia he had surmised on his arrival but a post-industrial, neo-pastoral feedlot. One species of human descendants—the vestige of the intelligentsia and leisure class—is pastured, kept unexercised and tender, and brought when still young and prime to the tables of those who were once their social and economic inferiors but are now society's go-getters and consumers. The fit survive; the pretty do not. The human race suffers both the after-effects of its own moral and political sins and the cold workings of biological politics, what the traveler calls "a law of nature we overlook, that intellectual versatility is the compensation for change, danger, and trouble" (ch. 10/13).

In Wells's secular prophecy the human race is headed, if not swiftly yet inevitably, toward bifurcation into one species of willful, pampered children lacking either responsibility or energy and another species, manually dextrous and enterprising but shut out from the sweetness and light that add graceful relief to the struggle for survival. The human stock, thus weakened, is ready for extinction. In his assessment of the Eloi and Morlocks, the traveler moves at last beyond culturally defined aversions and sympathies to an elegiac farewell to *homo sapiens*: "I grieved to think how brief the dream of the human intellect had been. It had committed suicide. It had set itself steadfastly towards comfort and ease, a balanced society with security and permanency as its watchword, it had attained its hopes—to come to this at last" (ch. 10/13). It is a verdict one might expect to find in that favorite of Wells's youthful reading, the definitive neoclassical pronouncement on the vanity of mind, Samuel Johnson's *Rasselas*.

The human lesson of 802,701 is raised to a cosmic one in "The Further Vision" the traveler receives as he rushes ahead in time. "Drawn on by the mystery of the earth's fate" (ch. 11/14), he watches the sun turn orange and then dull red as the solar system cools down. The earth's orbit begins to collapse; the sun fills one-tenth of the blackened sky; the atmosphere grows thin and windless; ice floats on the nearly motionless sea; seacoasts erode and the traveler's machine no longer comes to rest in the Thames valley but on a naked, pink, salt-encrusted beach. During the last phases of his journey, riding forward in bursts of a thousand years, he seldom leaves the saddle of his machine. The humanoid presence on the planet vanishes and the spectacle of human inadequacy and failure yields to what the physicist calls entropy and the prophet, apocalypse.

Near the end, the traveler watches the sun eclipsed by Mercury and a pall of darkness spread over the earth, omen of the coming final extinction of light. "The whole earth had become a garden," he thought in the first flush of his arrival in the false Eden of the Eloi (ch. 4/6). By the time he reaches the year 30 million, he sees the earth become a still wasteland. What he names the "abominable desolation" (ch. 11/14) on the shores of what was once England echoes the "abomination of desolation" prophesied in the New Testament Gospels:

> But in those days, after that tribulation, the sun shall be darkened, and the moon shall not give her light, and the stars of heaven shall fall, and the powers that are in heaven shall be shaken. And then shall they see the Son of man coming in the clouds with great power and glory (Mark 13 : 24-27).

The vision at the end of *The Time Machine* has the finality of the Christian apocalypse without its consolation. The Wellsian vision, scrupulously scientific, a matter of the logic of nature, has all—and more—of Mark's cosmic disasters. But there is no Son of man. Man's diminished progeny had long since died out to be replaced by giant crustaceans roaming the beaches during the world's latter days. And there is no power and glory: only the unedifying sight of a floppy, tentacular polyp in its death throes and a man from the nineteenth century sickening and fainting as he watches it. And so the world moves toward its end with, as T. S. Eliot would say three decades later, "a whimper," an ending witnessed neither by man nor by god.

The traveler returns to London, tells his story to a politely skeptical audience, and thereafter disappears. We do not learn where he traveled next in time, to what purpose, or with what results. The endings of the voyages and the voyager's life are left inconclusive. But in every other respect *The Time Machine* is a tale about endings. Though Wells was too self-consciously non-religious to say "Repent!" the effect of this fictional speculation is to urge the reader: The end *is* coming! Beware. Adapt. Reflect. The humanoid Eloi and Morlocks are the distant but direct consequences of the conditions of human life in 1895. The division between worker and manager, between upstairs and downstairs, between underground man and high society may seem only a political abstraction, or an ideological construct, or a sociological formula, but it will become a biological fact. Politics shall become flesh. That is the cautionary dimension of *The Time Machine*. But the future of the human race will depend not only on our choices but on inevitabilities more than human—on geological, zoological, meteorological, astronomical processes beyond the reach of merely human politics. *The Time Machine* proposes a long view of cosmic inhospitableness and of the inexorability of those forces that will neither respect human successes nor forgive human failings though they will have the final say on the duration of our civilization and our habitat.

But the cosmic perspective raises several final questions: where, at last, does Wells leave human choice and action? If apocalypse is inevitable, is the upshot of *The Time Machine* despair? Must we play the tragic, or worse, the melodramatic role? The traveler's friend, who appends an epilogue to the narrative of adventures and visions, suggests a way through the dilemma of how to use our knowledge of the future. We must adopt, he suggests, a hypothetical reality in which we tame our knowledge in order to act productively. Contrasting his own pragmatic perspective with the secular predestination of the traveler, the author of the epilogue says his friend "thought but cheerlessly of the Advancement of Mankind, and saw in the growing pile of civilization only a foolish heaping that must inevitably fall back upon and destroy its makers. If that is so, it remains for us to live as though it were not so." With an awareness of the finitude of our lives and the planet's life, we may yet act meaningfully, even heroically, within the limitations of our future, knowing that our thoughts and actions have human and planetary consequences, if not eternal consequences. *The Time Machine* belongs to that central body of morally affirmative speculative literature whose chief human counsel is not surrender but modesty.

NOTES

1. Where Wordsworth describes the visionary capacity of minds

   > By sensible impressions not enthralled,
   > But by their quickening impulse made more prompt
   > To hold fit converse with the spiritual world
   > And with the generations of mankind
   > Spread over time, past, present, and to come,
   > Age after age, till Time shall be no more.
   > —*The Prelude* (1850), XIV, ll. 106-111

2. How much Weena reveals about the traveler's fantasies and how much about the sentimentalities of Wells's imagination is, at the least, problematic. The women characters in Wells's science fiction are artistically negligible and ideologically embarrassing—when they are present at all. And the discussion of women in *A Modern Utopia* (ch. 6) is the least attractive section of an otherwise enlightened sociology.

IV
THE ISLAND OF DR. MOREAU AND THE INVISIBLE MAN

In subject and form the two important works Wells produced in 1896 and 1897 are complementary achievements. Both are grim imaginative cartoons, as the formal descriptions Wells gave them indicate; to *The Invisible Man* he appended the subtitle *A Grotesque Romance* and, in a preface to the Atlantic edition of his works, he called *The Island of Dr. Moreau* a "theological grotesque." Wells's two grotesques are the most macabre of his longer fictions and perhaps the most heartrending. Pain is depicted spectacularly in *Moreau* in the beast-men fashioned by an advanced but perverse surgical technique. *The Invisible Man* invites more intimate responses as Wells probes the anguish that is both motive for and symptom of the invisibility of a self-described "experimental investigator." In both books Wells uses the explicit depiction of suffering to explore the potential for horror in the scientific enterprise, the interface between investigation and obsession, the destructiveness of Moreau's "passion for research" and the invisible man's "passion for discovery" when such passions are unrestrained by human sympathy or intellectual discipline.

A.

Barring the men in the lifeboat and aboard the trading ship *Ipecacuanha* in the early chapters—men more beastly than human in impression—there are only three characters in *The Island of Dr. Moreau*, if one counts only human beings as characters. There is, of course, an abundance of varied beast-folk (including one who has a name) but their status as human creatures, as "characters," is at issue throughout the narrative. The indisputable characters are Dr. Moreau, his assistant Montgomery, and the shipwrecked narrator Prendick who finds himself an unwelcome guest on Moreau's Pacific island. All are trained biologists. The use of such coincidence is a prerogative of fable, and *Moreau* is a didactic fable about science and the modern world and about the human abuse of the scientific endeavor. Each of the three biologists, by deeds and intellectual stance, contributes to the fable's exploration of the powers, limits, and responsibilities of experimental researchers.

Moreau, the brilliant scholar and surgeon, is a portrait of

intellectual conceit, modeling himself on the divine pattern as a creator and law-giver. He views himself, by virtue of his expertise and imaginative boldness, as superior to other men and therefore exempt from the normal canons of judgment. "You cannot imagine," he tells Prendick, "the strange colourless delight of these intellectual desires. The thing before you is no longer an animal, a fellow-creature, but a problem" (ch. 14). Having been hounded out of England when his experiments on animals caused a public furor, Moreau set up shop on a remote island—the conventional retreat for both exiles and utopists—an island Edenic in its lush, tropical vegetation, but one which comes to seem a microcosm of the larger, and fallen, world. Moreau himself describes his island in the antiseptic language of the researcher as "a biological station—of a sort" (ch. 6), but in the more ominous language of fable he calls his locked operating room "a kind of Bluebeard's Chamber, in fact" (ch. 7). Combining the technical genius of the modern surgeon with the brutal ethos of Bluebeard, Moreau confidently asserts that the business of the scientific investigator is, and should be, amoral: "To this day I have never troubled about the ethics of the matter. The study of Nature makes a man at last as remorseless as Nature" (ch. 14).

Moreau's alcoholic aide Montgomery committed some unnamed crime while a medical student in London. Professionally ruined, he is doomed to be nothing more than a factotum to the only man who will have him, the banished vivisectionist. But humiliation and brandy do not entirely destroy Montgomery's sensibilities or his value as an interpreter of events on the island. Montgomery is Wells's chief vehicle for getting the reader beyond the visceral horror the beast-people inspire to the pathos of their miserable existence on Moreau's sufferance. Starved of human contact and patronized by Moreau, Montgomery seeks companionship and affection among the island's surgical anomalies. He even adopts one anthropoid creature, whom he calls M'ling, as his personal valet—and pet. At times tender, at times abusive towards M'ling, Montgomery displays, as Prendick comes to perceive, "a sneaking kindness" and "a vicious sympathy" for the beast-folk (ch. 15). Because he is himself a desperate failure, Montgomery can make us poignantly aware of the deep failure that underlies Moreau's surgical ingenuity. He is the spokesman for the victims of research and a spokesman all the more eloquent since he participates, helplessly, guiltily, cruelly, in their victimization.

Prendick's perspectives—the most important for the reader not only because he is our narrator but because he is an outsider—are more complicated. Though he loathes the screams that emanate from Moreau's operating room and shudders at the sight of some of the deformities that inhabit the island, Prendick is able to appreciate the grandeur of Moreau's ambitions. Recalling the dishonest and narrow-minded crusade in England against Moreau's work, Prendick makes a sardonic appraisal of journalists who arouse "the conscience of the nation" against scientists and an indictment of the academic community's timid silence. But he also offers an astute glimpse into the Faustian obsession of

Moreau:

> It was not the first time that conscience has turned against the methods of research. That doctor was simply howled out of the country. It may be he deserved to be, but I still think the tepid support of his fellow investigators and his desertion by the great body of scientific workers, was a shameful thing. Yet some of his experiments, by the journalist's account, were wantonly cruel. He might perhaps have purchased his social peace by abandoning his investigations, but he apparently preferred the latter, as most men would who have once fallen under the overmastering spell of research (ch. 7).

This is probably the most evenhanded interpretation that could be made of Moreau's behavior; Prendick does not allow his understanding of Moreau's predicament to pass into approval or tolerance of his surgical practices. Because he can discern no purpose to the experiments, no benefit to man or animal other than the gratification of Moreau's own curiosity, Prendick judges the research unethical and the researcher pathological.

Despite some shrewd analysis, Prendick is not always a very attractive narrator. He can be dense, self-serving, and inclined to hysteria (particularly in the early weeks when he assumes, incorrectly, that Moreau is transforming men into animals). Further, Prendick's conduct, especially toward the wretched Montgomery, is at times unspeakably priggish; the reader is not entirely out of sympathy when, in the final drunken spree before his death, Montgomery berates him as a "logic-chopping, chalky-faced saint of an atheist" (ch. 19). There is some of Swift's self-absorbed and knuckleheaded Gulliver in Prendick; he is so much given to interpreting with his imagination and his imagination is so susceptible to distortion that at the end of his stay on the island he is, like Gulliver, unable to readjust to urban life among *homo sapiens*. Prendick becomes pathological himself, seeing the mark of the animal in every human visage and turning London into a city of zombies:

> I would go out into the streets to fight with my delusion, and prowling women would mew after me, furtive craving men glance jealously at me, weary pale workers go coughing by me with tired eyes and eager paces like wounded deer dripping blood, old people, bent and dull, pass murmuring to themselves and all unheeding a ragged tail of gibing children. Then I would turn aside into some chapel, and even there, such was my disturbance, it seemed that the preacher gibbered Big Thinks even as the Ape Man had done; or into some lbirary, and there the intent faces over the books seemed but patient creatures waiting for prey. Particularly nauseous were the blank expressionless faces of people in trains and

omnibuses; they seemed no more my fellow-creatures than dead bodies would be, so that I did not dare to travel unless I was assured of being alone. And even it seemed that I, too, was not a reasonable creature, but only an animal tormented with some strange disorder in its brain, that sent it to wander alone like a sheep stricken with the gid (ch. 22).

While Prendick's psychiatric malady does not undercut the accuracy of his ethical critique of Moreau, it does jar the reader into an awareness of the fragility of the rule of reason. Prendick's self-image as a tormented animal is the final stage of a descent that had accelerated in the eight solitary months he spent as the only human inhabitant of the island after the deaths of Moreau and Montgomery. "I became one among the Beast People," Prendick reflects (ch. 21)—and we may reflect how Prendick's experience suggests the tentativeness of human civilization and of man's dominion over the beasts of the field. Nearly forty years after he wrote it, Wells remembered *The Island of Dr. Moreau* as "an exercise in youthful blasphemy" and as "my vision of the aimless torture in creation." Its blasphemy resides in its intimations of man's beastliness, of a world without a rationale, of sentient beings in pain afflicted by an indifferent doctor who neither loves nor hates the creatures he produces.

As a "theological grotesque" the book is, in part, parodic of Christian theology, with Moreau functioning as an avatar of the righteous Old Testament God—stern, patriarchal, legalistic. Prendick sees in the mutilated beings that emerge from the operating room "horrible caricatures of my Maker's image" (ch. 17). Moreau imposes on his creatures a reign of terror with whip and pistol and a ritual code of commandments the beast people are required to recite, though they can neither comprehend its principles nor fully adhere to its injunctions. And however much Prendick may feel disgust for Moreau's ideology and tactics, once Moreau is killed in a revolt by some of his creatures, Prendick is quick to realize the expedience of setting up a new cult around the departed Moreau.

In a parody of New Testament religion, Prendick implicates himself in Moreau's grotesque theology. To tame the beast folk and save his own skin, he turns priest and issues doctrines manufactured out of the Christian mythos of resurrection, transfiguration, and ascension into heaven. Addressing the community of beast-folk in front of Moreau's corpse, Prendick echoes Christ's words to his disciples: "A little while and ye shall not see me: and again, a little while, and ye shall see me" (John 16:16):

> "Children of the Law," I said, "he is *not* dead."
> M'ling turned his sharp eyes on me. "He has changed his shape—he has changed his body," I went on. "For a time you will not see him. He is...there"—I pointed upward—"where he can watch you. You cannot see him.

But he can see you. Fear the Law" (ch. 18).

The myth seems cruelly ironic, applied to the doctor who has painfully changed the shapes and bodies of these "children" of the god Moreau.

But Prendick's new religion fails. Some of the beast-people remain sullen and restless. Many are doubtful about the new cult. Some eventually lose interest in it. A few, notably a Dog-Man, fall in with Prendick's myth in a brainless sort of way, eager for consolation and something to be loyal to. At last Prendick is left merely with a pooch's sycophancy as the only achievement of his evangelism. That is Wells's mischievously blasphemous verdict on the intellectual durability of the Judeo-Christian legacy.

But *Moreau* isn't merely a burlesque of theology; there is a theological vision in the romance, though a grotesque and un-Christian one. The book is a study in sin—sin as a Darwinian evolutionist or Huxleyan ecologist might define it. Like his great literary predecessor Victor Frankenstein, Moreau offends against nature. In Mary Shelley's romance, Frankenstein tries to bypass sexuality and the feminine in a grotesque act of parthenogenesis; the child he produces is a monster—not the thing of beauty he fantasized, but a wrinkled, oversized, jaundiced, pathetic piece of stitchwork. Similarly, Moreau violates the natural process by trying to take an evolutionary shortcut. Presumptuously, he conceives of himself as a sculptor of flesh and exalts surgery not as a science of healing but as an outlet for "the artistic turn of mind." Yet the products of his handiwork are always ghastly to behold, as he admits:

> Sometimes I rise above my level, sometimes I fall below it, but always I fall short of the things I dream. The human shape I can get now, almost with ease, so that it is lithe and graceful, or thick and strong; but often there is trouble with the hands and claws—painful things that I dare not shape too freely. But it is in the subtle grafting and reshaping one must needs do to the brain that my trouble lies. The intelligence is often oddly low, with unaccountable blank ends, unexpected gaps. And least satisfactory of all is something that I cannot touch, somewhere—I cannot determine where—in the seat of the emotions (ch. 14).

Moreau recognizes his failures, but interpreting them as mere technical deficiencies he refuses to grasp their implications. The three areas he lists as failures are the areas which —much more than physical form—are most central to the definition of the human species: prehensile hands, a highly-developed brain, emotional intricacy and range. In addition, Moreau hasn't been able to create anthropoids who reproduce human or even humanesque offspring. All the progeny of his beast folk revert to their original genetic material; only a few survive and they must be surgically altered. Moreau excuses his failures on the ground that he has been engaged on the project for a short time, but his justification is, ironically, an indictment of his research: "After all," he says, "what is ten years? Man has been a hundred thousand in the making" (ch. 14). Exactly. The arduous process of natural selection—over millennia—is usurped by Moreau in his effort to get a quick fix on nature. The natural suffering of adaptation and survival is replaced by the artificial—and gratuitous—pain of Moreau's surgical instruments. At the cost of torture and a lifetime of suffering the creatures exist to flatter the ego of their creator, though they remain but poor, botched specimens of his finite skills. Prendick makes the leap from Moreau's delusions of godhead to a comprehensive theology of suffering when he interprets the screams he hears day after day from a puma on the operating table: "It was as if all the pain in the world had found a voice" (ch. 8). Moreau's island is a miniature of the world—the world as shaped and afflicted by the arrogance of the human presence and as suffering from the absence of a merciful god.

The Island of Dr. Moreau is not simply an antivivisectionist tract or a gruesome horror story as early reviewers of this most disturbing and least popular of Wells's youthful romances charged. We can now see it as an early, articulate, imaginative fable about the felonious consequences of an unbridled humanism, about what happens when a man forgets that he too is an animal and affects to be a god. Even now one can hardly talk about the rights of animals without inviting snickers or being thought a crank. [1] But Prendick teaches us, through his observations of the protracted agony of the beast-folk, the horror of taking the human form as the pattern to which all of nature should be cut. If we fail to respect the integrity of our fellow, sentient, nonhuman inhabitants of the planet, we fail to justify our ascendancy as the dominant species. And, it goes without saying, the arrogance that dictates the effort to alter beasts to men is part and parcel of the madness that attempts to exterminate or subjugate or brutalize human beings classified as unfit or imperfect or incompatible. It is but a short step from Moreau's island to the Nazi death camps and the prisons of South Africa.

Wells may have been more explicitly prophetic in *A Modern Utopia*, which foresees the possible horrors of "national harrowing and reaping machines, and race-destroying fumigations" (10:5). But there is not a more chilling moment in Wells's science fiction than Prendick's meditation on the effects of Moreau's surgery. While it is addressed specifically to man's relationship to animals, the passage cannot help but confirm our knowledge of how human beings have defiled other members of their own species and of the too-durable legacy of colonialist and missionary obsession:

> Poor Brutes! I began to see the viler aspect of Moreau's cruelty. I had not thought before of the pain and trouble that came to these poor victims after they

had passed from Moreau's hands. I had shivered only at the days of actual torment in the enclosure. But now that seemed to be the lesser part. Before they had been beasts, their instincts fitly adapted to their surroundings, and happy as living things may be. Now they stumbled in the shackles of humanity, living in a fear that never died, fretted by a law they could not understand; their mock-human existence began in an agony, was one long internal struggle, one long dread of Moreau—and for what? It was the wantonness that stirred me (ch. 16).

B.

The wantonness of research, the arrogance of mind in *The Invisible Man* emanate from a wholly different source. The protagonist is no mature, self-confident, renowned, elegant man like Dr. Moreau, but an emphatically young man named Griffin, a premedical student and winner of the chemistry medal at University College in London, who abandons medicine and chemistry for a single-minded, private study of physics and optics. "You know what fools we are at two and twenty?" he asks later, reflecting on his abandonment of a promising medical career (ch. 19). Fascinated by the properties of light and seduced by the notion of turning his knowledge to power, he becomes as obsessive as Moreau. Both the invisible man and the vivisectionist are scientific prodigies who become social outcasts. Griffin, however, lacks not only Moreau's doctorate but his forethought, discipline, and emotional detachment. While Moreau prides himself on his isolation, Griffin is tormented by his. Moreau the unflappable professional is the temperamental opposite of the "aggressive and explosive" Griffin (ch. 3). A few moments of spirited hijinks aside, the experiment by which Griffin makes himself invisible is a thorough disaster, begun in excruciating pain and concluding in mayhem, insanity, and mob lynching.

Moreau is intrigued by the *idea* of research; he is the "pure" researcher (so-called), uninterested in the application or utility of his experiments, unmoved by the suffering of his surgical sculptures. But Griffin is motivated by the advantages he supposes will accrue to him when invisible; he treats his science as alchemy, aiming "to transcend magic" and attain "the mystery, the power, the freedom" of invisibility. Pure or disinterested investigation he views with contempt: "As though Knowing could be any satisfaction to a man!" (ch. 19) As simultaneous researcher and subject of research, victim and beneficiary of the experiment in invisibility, Griffin is also the voice of suffering as much as the embodiment of ambition. Indifferent to the anguish of others (including his father's suicide, for which he bears large responsibility), he is acutely susceptible to pain himself. The process of bleaching the color from his blood cells nearly drives him crazy with pain: "I had not expected the suffering. A night of racking anguish, sickness and fainting. I set my teeth, though my skin was presently afire, all my body afire; but I lay there like grim death" (ch. 20). The cry of Moreau's puma is re-echoed in Griffin's sobbing and wailing and groaning that punctuate the entire narrative of *The Invisible Man*. And as Moreau's animals go under the knife to emerge as "horrible caricatures" of the human form, so Griffin invisible becomes "a swathed and bandaged caricature of a man" (ch. 23).

The description of the transformation of Griffin into the invisible man in his makeshift laboratory is a typical but splendid Wellsian metamorphosis. [2] It is preceded by the obligatory gesture of "domesticating" the idea of corporeal invisibility, but that explanation—a matter of fast gab about optics and the physiology of blood cells—is deferred until two-thirds of the way into the narrative. The effect of the postponement is to allow the reader to experience the fantastic impression the invisible Griffin makes with something of the astonishment, if not the naive superstition, of the villagers of Iping in the first dozen chapters.

When the invisible man arrives in Iping at the end of the winter, the event amounts to an extraordinary eruption of the fantastic into the quotidian world of rural England: "Thus it was that on the twenty-ninth day of February, at the beginning of the thaw, this singular person fell out of infinity into Iping Village" (ch. 3). [3] Until chapter 17 when the invisible man encounters his old acquaintance Dr. Kemp, reveals his name to be Griffin, and recounts the events leading up to his present condition, the narrative is largely a mixture of mystery and deft social comedy. We watch the villagers' efforts at detection and deduction as they try out various hypotheses about the bandaged and muffled figure in their midst: he's a fugitive from justice, a half-breed, an anatomical freak, a lunatic, an anarchist, a bogeyman. However fatuous some of the guesses, the simple presence of the mysterious visitor upsets routine and dominates gossip in Iping. Children who bump into him have nightmares; adults are perplexed, angered, and intimidated by him; teenagers nervously mimic him, skulking behind him on his outings with their collars up and their hatbrims pulled down.

Only after the vicar's house is robbed and the evidence points to the strange guest at the inn do the villagers—and particularly Mrs. Hall the innkeeper—overcome their shyness and fear to confront Griffin. In terror Mrs. Hall watches him uncover his face and become "metamorphosed" before her eyes as he hands her his rubber nose and forces her to look into the empty cavity where she expects a face to be. "It was worse than anything" (ch. 7). Worse than peculiar or morbid or immoral, the stranger defies both nature and convention. He is a ghost with flesh. An animate vacancy with a mean temper and muscular energy. And, not least important in this small-town milieu, a crude, troublesome guest who insults his hosts, repels their curiosity, and can't pay his bills. Desperate to regain control over their

37

little world, the villagers invoke the comfortingly familiar remedy of the police and send a constable armed with a warrant to arrest the invisible man. In a grotesquely comic scene reminiscent of the escape of another mysterious young man surrounded by arresting officers, the invisible man strips and eludes them. His analogue is the anonymous youth following Jesus in the garden of Gethsemane: "And there followed him a certain young man, having a linen cloth cast about his naked body; and the young men laid hold on him: And he left the linen cloth and fled from them naked" (Mark 14: 51-52).

The often broadly comic first section of *The Invisible Man* is not irrelevant to the revelations and explanations which emerge in the last third. In the first sixteen chapters, the evidence accumulates that to be invisible is to be isolated, angry, on the run, impotent, naked to one's enemies. We see the invisible man in relationship with three other important characters: Mrs. Hall, the inquisitive, grumpy innkeeper; Thomas Marvel, the tramp and con man who becomes his unwilling accomplice in petty theft; and Dr. Kemp, the sophisticated and morally inert scientist to whom Griffin tells his story and by whom he is betrayed. But there is no real social connection between Griffin and the others; they are his antagonists and, in the long run, command more power than he does. Describing the solitary midnight experiments that led to his transformation, he tells Kemp, "I was alone....In all my great moments I have been alone" (ch. 19).

Long before he becomes the mysterious alien dropped from infinity into Iping Village, Griffin was an alienated student in London, a bored and ill-paid teacher in the boondocks, a secretive apartment-dweller thought odd and maybe dangerous by his landlord and neighbors. Born an albino and grown into a friendless and irritable recluse, Griffin was already *an* invisible man before he became *the* Invisible Man. That is one implication of the fevered dream he has in the Omnium department store where he hides on the first night of his invisibility. He dreams he is back at his father's funeral where the mourners cannot see that he is being buried alive:

> "You also," said a voice, and suddenly I was being forced towards the grave. I struggled, shouted, appealed to the mourners, but they continued stonily following the service; the old clergyman, too, never faltered droning and sniffing through the ritual. I realised I was invisible and inaudible, that overwhelming forces had their grip on me. I struggled in vain, I was forced over the brink, the coffin rang hollow as I fell upon it, and the gravel came flying after me in spadefuls. Nobody heeded me, nobody was aware of me (ch. 22).

Griffin embraces esoteric research in the hope that it will finally get people to pay attention to him. It is his escape route: out of obscurity, out of the genteel poverty of his childhood, out of the humiliation of a wretchedly unsatisfying job. To make himself physically invisible, he imagines, is to abolish his past and acquire the freedom of a limitless future. But once transformed, Griffin finds a huge discrepancy between his fantasies of power and the new constraints of his physical condition. He must travel naked even in winter—and then mud or broken glass may still cause tell-tale footprints. He cannot eat around visible persons lest the undigested food in his stomach give him away. He lives in terror of the acute hearing and smell of blind men and dogs. He discovers he can move safely in human company only by enveloping every inch of his body in opaque coverings. And thus one of the bitterest ironies of his metamorphosis is that an invisible man must disguise himself as a visible one to hold body and soul together. When Griffin tries to lord it over the impressionable Thomas Marvel, Wells comically deflates his pretensions by calling attention to the naked, shivering, grippy body behind the lordly utterance: "'An invisible man is a man of power.' He stopped for a moment to sneeze violently" (ch. 9).

In those moments when he is still sane enough to assess his situation lucidly, Griffin perceives the gap between his fantasies and the fact of his vulnerability. While invisibility confers a few advantages, it entails a great many more liabilities than he had guessed. If Bluebeard is Dr. Moreau's ancestor in fable, than King Midas, whose golden touch frustrates rather than fulfills desire, is Griffin's mythic prototype. Griffin tells Kemp what "a helpless absurdity" he found himself on the very first day of his invisibility:

> Before I made this mad experiment I had dreamt of a thousand advantages. That afternoon it seemed all disappointment. I went over the heads of the things a man reckons desirable. No doubt invisibility made it possible to get them, but it made it impossible to enjoy them when they are got. Ambition—what is the good of pride of place when you cannot appear there? (ch. 23)

Griffin is too rich psychologically, too sensitive and self-conscious to be neatly pigeonholed in Dr. Kemp's definition of him as "pure selfishness" (ch. 25). While dangerous to himself and others, Griffin is a more complicated and engaging human being than the panicky doctor ever understands. The most pitiable feature of the invisible man's experience is the degree to which his experiment makes him mad—in both senses of the word. His insanity needs little commentary; as his disillusionment and desperation grow, his fragile mental control gives way until, on the last day of his life, he is consumed with plotting a Reign of Terror. His fantasies turn absurdly monarchist: "This is day one of year one of the new epoch—the Epoch of the Invisible Man. I am Invisible Man the First" (ch. 27). But it is not his lunacy that is so moving; it is his anger, his nearly uninterrupted irritability that is both symptom and effect of his obsession.

From the beginning we observe the rage that eats Griffin up. To the Iping villagers, he looks "like a lobster" (ch. 2) and "like an angry diving-helmet" (ch. 7) in his strange clothing, stolen from a theatrical costumer, and his blue-tinted spectacles. His behavior, we are often reminded, is chronically frantic and "his manner was that of a man suffering under almost unendurable provocation" (ch. 4). Throughout the narrative we see him smashing things up—bottles, heads, the electrical apparatus in his apartment, crockery in the Omnium, the booths at Iping's Whit-Monday Fair, the windows of the Coach and Horses Inn, the window in the bar of the Jolly Cricketers Inn, the windows and shutters and doors of Kemp's house. Unable to eat the lunch he has ordered in a London restaurant without risking his disguise, he transfers his anger at himself to the waiters: "I could have smashed the silly devils" (ch. 23). He at last arouses the organized hatred of the populace, having encountered the inoffensive Mr. Wicksteed on a lonely path and, in the characteristic manifestation of his rage, "attacked him, beat down his feeble defences, broke his arm, felled him, and smashed his head to a jelly" (ch. 26). In the end, brutally, he is smashed with a shovel and trampled under the feet of a mob of enraged citizens.

It is a fit though bloody conclusion to Griffin's short life, a life consumed with a self-destructive anger that invisibility was powerless magically to conceal or assuage. As visibility gradually returns to his corpse, bystanders watch flesh grow on the invisible nightmare that had haunted them. Into view comes "his crushed chest and his shoulders, and the dim outline of his drawn and battered features." At last, fully visible, "there lay, naked and pitiful on the ground, the bruised and broken body of a young man about thirty. His hair and beard were white—not grey with age but white with the whiteness of albinism, and his eyes were like garnets. His hands were clenched, his eyes wide open, and his expression was one of anger and dismay" (ch. 28).

In some ways Griffin is more dreadful than Moreau: he murders; he breaks a child's ankle; he is a vandal, an arsonist, and, in his last days, a merciless terrorist. Moreau is always a gentleman, reserved, polite, cultivated—a soulless genius. By contrast, Griffin is an oaf and a hoodlum, an intelligent punk from the wrong side of the tracks, a born loser in spite of his ingenuity and ambition. His manners are awful; he carries an enormous chip on his shoulder; he is a malicious prankster; he spits out his hatreds—for the students he teaches, for his own professors, for his father, for Jews, for blacks, for old people, for the uneducated, for animals. Nevertheless, Wells manages to make him a figure who earns our pity and our charity while Moreau remains always a chilly, largely allegorical representation of a type of mind. Moreau is never laughable, but Wells permits us to laugh at Griffin and our laughter becomes the instrument for understanding the invisible man as a touching and fragile being.

Wells gives Griffin a private life and explains, as he chooses not to do with Moreau, what makes Griffin tick; he allows us inside his skin, inside his invisibility, inside his anguish.

The invisible man's first words, as he staggers cold, wet, and carefully muffled into the inn at Iping, are, "A fire, in the name of human charity!" His last words, as he is being beaten to death by vigilantes, are, "Mercy! Mercy!" Nowhere in the narrative are these cries for love and mercy answered. Instead, in the darkly comic epilogue we see the commercial exploitation of his tragedy; the tramp Marvel turns Griffin's horror into profit by devising music hall performances based on his exploits and by opening the Invisible Man Inn at Port Stowe. For all its grim horror, frequently exuberant comedy, and intense ethical debate (especially in the chapters with Kemp), at bottom *The Invisible Man* is a *cri de coeur* that demands of its readers an exercise in human sympathy. While it is often regarded as a smaller accomplishment than his other early romances, less extrapolative and more fantastic than the typical Wellsian fiction, the truth is that nowhere else in the early works does Wells create so vivid and moving a psychological study. Griffin is the finest, most engaging character in Wells's science fiction, an achievement often overlooked by Wells's critics but implicit in the famous letter Joseph Conrad wrote Wells after reading *The Invisible Man*:

> I suppose you'll have the common decency to believe me when I tell you I am always powerfully impressed by your work. Impressed is *the* word, O Realist of the Fantastic! whether you like it or not. And if you want to know what impresses me it is to see how you contrive to give over humanity into the clutches of the Impossible and yet manage to keep it down (or up) to its humanity, to its flesh, blood, sorrow, folly. *That* is the achievement! In this little book you do it with an appalling completeness.

NOTES

1. See Peter Singer's important argument in the unfortunately titled *Animal Liberation: A New Ethics for Our Treatment of Animals* (New York: New York Review, 1975), esp. ch. 5. If Singer's study seems too contemporary to shape a reading of *Moreau*, two of Wells's essays may be consulted—"The Province of Pain" (1894) and "Human Evolution, an Artificial Process" (1896), collected in *Early Writings*, ed. Philmus and Hughes (see Primary Materials, item I,B,6, at the back of this *Guide*).

2. For other examples of metamorphosis of persons and landscapes, see the reversions of Moreau's hybrids to their animal origins (*Moreau*, ch. 21); the lunar dawn in *First Men* (ch. 7); the aging of Mr. Eden in "The Story of the Late Mr. Elvesham";

the awakening of the earth in *In the Days of the Comet* (I,2:1); and Books I and II of *The Food of the Gods*.

3. The date of February 29 in the Atlantic edition text makes this passage inconsistent with the first sentence of ch. 1: "The stranger came early in February one wintry day...." Other editions, including the first and the 1934 reissue of the romances, make the calendar consistent by giving the date as February 9. Apparently in preparing the Atlantic text, Wells overlooked—or ignored—the inconsistency to achieve the symbolic effect of placing so unusual an event on an unusual date.

V
THE WAR OF THE WORLDS AND
THE FIRST MEN IN THE MOON

Wells's two interplanetary romances play out the fantasy of global civilizations encountering each other. In one, Mars launches a sneak attack against the earth; in the other, two terrestrial explorers penetrate the moon. Both adventures are instructive failures. Compelled by the urge to survive as their own diminished world cools, Wells's Martians gamble on attacking creatures they deem expendable inferiors; despite their military and technological superiority, the Martians are undone in the end by a basic ecological principle they overlooked. The two earthmen who fly to the moon do so out of disinterested curiosity (in the case of the physicist Cavor) and economic opportunism (in the case of Bedford, a ruined businessman with dreams of lunar gold mines). Their expedition fails out of sheer carelessness: Bedford manages to lose his spacecraft on an English beach while Cavor, who alone knows how to manufacture the vehicle's fuel, loses his life in the deep caves of the ant-like Selenites. Both narratives are glosses on the presumptions of colonialism. More generally, they undermine humanist pretensions by offering mordant commentaries on what Bedford calls "our incurable anthropomorphism." The epigraph Wells chose for *The War of the Worlds*, from the seventeenth-century German astronomer Johannes Kepler, is equally pertinent to *The First Men in the Moon*: "But who shall dwell in these worlds if they be inhabited?...Are we or they Lords of the World?...And how are all things made for man?"

A.

The War of the Worlds is narrated from a typical Wellsian perspective by a familiar Wellsian protagonist. As in the later romances of global catastrophe, *In the Days of the Comet*, *The War in the Air*, and *The World Set Free*, the history of war between Mars and Earth is offered some years after the fact by a narrator who looks back sadly, ironically, and with grave tolerance on the intellectual vanities and moral deficiencies of the recent human past. "A professed and recognised writer on philosophical themes" (II, 7), he has the authority to interpret the war. At the same time his history is not a philosophical exercise conducted from an ivory tower; he was a participant in the war—more accurately, a wayfarer through it—and his narrative has the vigorous authenticity of eyewitness testimony. Like the time traveler returning with his lame foot and bloody sock and withered flowers, like *The Island of Dr. Moreau*'s Prendick with his recurrent nightmares and agoraphobia, this narrator also bears the evidence of his harrowing experience: in the space of fifteen days as a virtual prisoner of war in a collapsed house, his hair turns completely gray. Beyond that physical sign, he also has nightmares—of the countryside in flames and of the empty, pestilential city—and the memory of how, under the stress of privation and imminent death, he killed a priest with an axe.

While the events recorded in *The War of the Worlds* are themselves thrilling, it is the voice and demeanor of this sober interpreter that compels our attention. The literary production of that voice is less a personal memoir than a *memento mori* for the human species, an intimation of our mortality. The narrator writes to provoke "the general reader" to share his own philosophical uncertainties, that "abiding sense of doubt and insecurity" which is, he believes, the important lesson of the invasion (II, 10). Because humanity should not mistake its "reprieve" from annihilation for victory, the war's end is cause for reflection rather than jubilation.

H. G. Wells's narrative (as opposed to the renowned radio adaptation by Orson Welles) is not a Hallowe'en prank designed to spook its audience. The splendidly conceived and depicted horrors—the moving tripods, the heat ray, the poisonous black smoke, and the molluscan Martians themselves—are not the imaginative center of the narrative; they are instrumental to the critical assessment of humanity Wells's narrator undertakes. We are given a dispassionate vision of pride and punishment by a trained philosophical mind, a mind capable of evaluating even its own subjective and intimate experience "from the outside, from somewhere inconceivably remote, out of time, out of space, out of the stress and tragedy of it all" (I, 7). While remaining thoroughly incarnate like all Wellsian narrators, the voice in *The War of the Worlds* foreshadows in mood and manner the famous "disembodied viewpoint" Olaf Stapledon invented to make his cold assessment of human civilization in *Star Maker* (1937).

Book I, "The Coming of the Martians," recounts the disruption—as much psychological as physical—of daily human activity and habits of mind by the shock of invasion, wholesale destruction, and enormous death tolls. In the face of calamity, human beings prove distressingly ineffectual. They respond with empty gestures of heroism, religious pieties, panic, selfish profiteering—or they do not react at all. The narrator notes the tendency of official histories of the war to exaggerate the initial public response to the death at Woking, where the first Martian cylinder falls. "All London was electrified by the news from Woking," he quotes one of them. But this *ex post facto* melodrama misrepresents the psychological realities. Most Londoners don't read newspapers anyway, the narrator reminds us, and those who do fail to grasp—or choose to insulate themselves from—the gravity of the news. Modern journalism makes even immediate danger seem stylized, fictional, routine: "The habit of personal security, moreover, is so deeply fixed in the Londoner's mind, and startling intelligence so much a matter of course in the papers, that they could read without any personal tremors" (I, 14). And while city dwellers urbanely munch the news with their breakfast toast, in the countryside vendors of apples and ginger-beer set up stalls to serve the villagers who gather around the smoking pit on Horsell Common to gawk at Woking's cylinder. [1]

Even after the cylinder opens to reveal its cargo of leathery, brown monsters from Mars, it takes people a while to appreciate the magnitude of what is happening. They imagine, at first, that they need only bring forward their cannon, their army, and their battleships. So strong is the British habit of empire that they cannot grasp that the Martians are the colonists and *homo sapiens* the inferior race. The history of territorial expansion by human adventurers furnished Wells with abundant analogues for the Martian invasion—notably, the genocide of native Tasmanians by British colonialists and the slaughter of the bison and the dodo by greedy human carnivores. In the early days of the invasion, the narrator himself fails to gauge the imperial ambitions and capacities of the Martians and assures his wife that the invaders will be a pushover once the army sends its best ammunition. Looking back six years later, he parodies his confidence with a grimly fantastic simile that points up the genocidal dimension of *The War of the Worlds*: "So some respectable dodo in the Mauritius might have lorded it in his nest, and discussed the arrival of that shipful of pitiless sailors in want of animal food. 'We will peck them to death to-morrow, my dear'" (I, 7).

The narrator's initial experience of the Martian assault is confined to the suburban villages southwest of London; the panic in the metropolis and the sea battle on the eastern coast are recorded by his brother, a medical student, in the interlude that occupies most of chapters 14-17 of Book I. When London is finally aroused to the threat against it, social institutions and moral constraints collapse. Along the roads, at the railway stations, on the docks, panic is the only rule. Rights of property are no longer recognized as refugees from London pillage rural granaries, and elementary decencies are subordinated to the cruelest expediencies of survival. The urban exodus becomes "a stampede," "a rout," "a massacre" (I, 17). The least edifying features of the human personality surface, its barbarism, its selfishness, even its silly parochialism, as in the ludicrous xenophobia of Mrs. Elphinstone whom the narrator's brother attempts to put on a boat out of the country: "She had never been out of England before, she would rather die than trust herself friendless in a foreign country, and so forth. She seemed, poor woman, to imagine that the French and the Martians might prove very similar" (I, 17).

While human inertia allows the invaders to reap the full advantage of their surprise attack, the keystone of the Martian strategy is the defeat of the anthropomorphizing imagination—our proud inclination to see all reality in human terms, as designed

45

for human ends, as wearing ultimately a human face. The newspapers articulate that humanist bias with their inaccurate headlines: "Men from Mars!" (I, 8). But the bystander in Woking who keeps repeating, "What ugly *brutes*! Good God! What ugly brutes!" (I, 5) in mixed disbelief, horror, and condescension is an even fitter emblem of human pride. That *homo sapiens* might be subject to a race of what appear to be godforsaken brutes is more than the (white, Anglo-Saxon, Christian) populace of Wells's fiction can take. Physically, the Martians are an affront to the human species. Not *men* from Mars but "boilers on stilts" (I, 14), as one policeman describes them in their hundred-foot-high fighting machines. The narrator's anatomically scrupulous rendition of a Martian he observed at first hand contains a lengthy, precise inventory of its non-human characteristics:

> They were, I now saw, the most unearthly creatures it is possible to conceive. They were huge round bodies—or, rather, heads—about four feet in diameter, each body having in front of it a face. This face had no nostrils—indeed, the Martians do not seem to have had any sense of smell—but it had a pair of very large, dark-coloured eyes, and just beneath this a kind of fleshy beak. In the back of this head or body—I scarcely know how to speak of it—was the single tight tympanic surface, since known to be anatomically an ear, though it must have been almost useless in our denser air. In a group round the mouth were sixteen slender, almost whip-like tentacles, arranged in two bunches of eight each....
> Strange as it may seem to a human being, all the complex apparatus of digestion, which makes up the bulk of our bodies, did not exist in the Martians. They were heads—merely heads. Entrails they had none. They did not eat, much less digest. Instead, they took the fresh, living blood of other creatures, and *injected* it into their own veins. I have myself seen this being done, as I shall mention in its place. But, squeamish as I may seem, I cannot bring myself to describe what I could not endure even to continue watching. Let it suffice to say, blood obtained from a still living animal, in most cases from a human being, was run directly by means of a little pipette into the recipient canal (II, 2).

While the language of this description retains the "photographically distinct" clarity (I, 7) that is this romance's stylistic hallmark, the Martians are so alien in appearance and behavior that they challenge the narrator's powers of conceptualization and exposition. "Let it suffice to say," "I cannot bring myself to describe," "I scarcely know how to speak," he protests, because the linguistic habits of an anthropomorphizing imagination subvert dispassionate classification. He struggles to keep his nausea under control and maintain his clinical stance, but when he italicizes *injected* the note of hysteria arising from the assault on human sensibilities is almost palpable. He at last bypasses the details of the vampiric draining of a human victim and settles for an analogy: "The bare idea of this is no doubt horribly repulsive to us, but at the same time I think that we should remember how repulsive our carnivorous habits would seem to an intelligent rabbit." Martian anatomy, like Martian intelligence in the opening paragraph of the romance, is so surpassingly different from its human counterpart and yet so disconcertingly analogical in function that it can best be understood in proportional terms. Martians : men :: men : the beasts that perish.

Under the terror of the Martian occupation in Book II, *Homo sapiens* is often likened to rabbits, ants, and rats. All are animals we often think of in social terms, in dense throngs breeding and multiplying, panicky and confused when their community is violated. But each species also has its distinctive resonance for us: rabbits are timid, ants are puny, rats are nasty. The associations are not flattering to their human analogues in Book II. One of the most impressive comparisons is made by the narrator, surveying the ravaged landscape as he emerges from his fifteen-day imprisonment at Sheen:

> For that moment I touched an emotion beyond the common range of men, yet one that the poor brutes we dominate know only too well. I felt as a rabbit might feel returning to his burrow and suddenly confronted by the work of a dozen busy navvies digging the foundations of a house. I felt the first inkling of a thing that presently grew quite clear in my mind, that oppressed me for many days, a sense of dethronement, a persuasion that I was no longer a master, but an animal among the animals, under the Martian heel. With us it would be as with them, to lurk and watch, to run and hide; the fear and empire of man had passed away (II, 6).

When the narrator meets an artilleryman on the road to London—a man he first encountered in Woking early in the war—the animal metaphors multiply. The artilleryman foresees earth under Martian rule becoming a hell "built for rabbits" with "nice roomy cages, fattening food, careful breeding, no worry." He constructs an elaborate Morlockian fantasy of guerilla warfare in which a tough, unsubmissive human remnant takes to the London sewers to survive, grows cunning, and sabotages the above-ground regime. "The risk," he acknowledges, "is that we who keep wild will go savage—degenerate into a sort of big, savage rat." But even that scenario is preferable to the alternative of meek surrender, to becoming the Martians' slaves and fodder: "eatable ants" (II, 7). Although the narrator eventually recognizes the soldier's bravado as energetic but hollow role-playing, the animal analogues remain suggestive interpretive devices. *The War of the Worlds* is too complex a text to be reduced to a vegetarian or anticolonialist or pacifist or any other kind of "message," but one lesson that impresses itself on the philosophic narrator is his new conviction that man is not lord of creation but "an inferior animal." "Surely," he says, deriving an ethical principle from his own brief experience as a trapped animal surrounded by Martian predators, "if we have learned nothing else, this war has taught us pity—pity for those witless souls that suffer our dominion" (II, 7).

In the Book of Genesis, Adam is granted the authority to name the animals and thereby the right of rule over them. In *The War of the Worlds* human authority and rights are questioned, and the narrator plays a distinctly anti-Adamic role. In the climactic chapters of Book II, as he moves in eerie silence through dead London, "the great Mother of Cities" (II, 8), he imagines himself "the last man left alive" (II, 6), Adam's obverse. [2] The religious accent grows heavier as the narrative progresses, though Wells is characteristically harsh on those expressions of religious enthusiasm or consolation that strike him as soft or easy. When the narrator first meets the self-indulgent curate after the Martians have demonstrated their heat ray by destroying the town of Weybridge, he is put off by the priest's spluttering references to Sodom and Gomorrah and his facile despair in the face of a supposedly divine judgment: "What good is religion if it collapses under calamity? Think of what earthquakes and floods, wars and volcanoes, have done before to men! Did you think God had exempted Weybridge? He is not an insurance agent" (I, 13). Later when they are trapped together at Sheen, the curate's hysteria becomes a life-threatening madness and the narrator must kill him before his manic preaching alerts the Martians to their presence.

The curate's brand of religious expression is treated with contempt as a merely rhetorical buffer between man and his suffering, as the shamming of "timorous, anaemic, hateful souls, full of shifty cunning who face neither God nor man, who face not even themselves" (II, 3). But the skeptical narrator is eventually moved to make room for a divine explanation for the death of the Martians and the salvation of his own planet. Speaking as a scientific observer, he sees the felling of the Martians by bacterial microorganisms as natural and inevitable, a corollary of Darwinian biology: "By the toll of a billion deaths man has bought his birthright of the earth, and it is his against all comers; it would still be his were the Martians ten times as mighty as they are" (II, 8). But this rationalist's tribute to human hegemony and terrestrial ecology is qualified by the narrator's burst of spontaneous piety in attributing the *existence* of the germs to a benevolent, creating deity: "after all man's devices had failed," the Martians are slain "by the humblest things that God, in his wisdom, has put upon this earth" (II, 8).

As he wanders the streets of London alone, surveying the great empty tripods, the half-built flying machine, and the corpses of the Martian vanguard, the narrator ponders the mystery of the invasion's sudden ending and is torn between reason and faith, between the scientific and the miraculous interpretations. Climbing to the summit of Primrose Hill—the appropriate terrain for spiritual vision—and observing in prospect the ruins of London that will soon be rebuilt, he yields to the religious impulse and stands "weeping and praising God" (II, 9). It is an odd, though powerful, moment in the romance. When the narrator draws his conclusions about the invasion in the epilogue, the spiritual language falls away and he becomes once more the philosopher and scientist. Perhaps we are to see the spirituality of chapters 8 and 9 as a momentary lapse into primitive feeling under stress. Or, perhaps, that episode demonstrates the viability of the Judeo-Christian tradition in providing myths to explain the inexplicable and a language for coming to terms with events so massive or overwhelming or horrible that they are otherwise unspeakable.

Human losses and recoveries, whether miraculous or inevitable, are not the only concerns of the final chapters. Indeed, one of the ironies of the ending of *The War of the Worlds* is that the dying ululation of the last Martian on Earth is far more moving than the narrator's return to Woking and reunion with his lost wife. (It would be convenient to believe Wells intended this irony, but the effect more likely has something to do with his usual inability to create female characters or to represent marital love convincingly.) The haunting, thoroughly alien death-wail the narrator repeatedly hears piercing the silence of London, "Ulla, ulla, ulla, ulla"—"a sobbing alternation of two notes" (II, 8)—has the conviction of truth, signaling tragic overreaching on the Martians' part. The narrator's discovery in the penultimate chapter of his pale, fainting wife at the French window of his abandoned house is, by contrast, stale with banality:

> And there, amazed and afraid, even as I stood amazed and afraid, were my cousin and my wife—my wife white and tearless. She gave a faint cry.
> "I came," she said. "I knew—knew——"
> She put her hand to her throat—swayed. I made a step forward, and caught her in my arms (II, 9).

A made-for-TV movie could have done no worse.

But even a flawed ending does not cancel the book's point, first made in the opening paragraph and reiterated in the view from the narrator's study window of the fiery demolition of Woking on the night the fighting began, that ours is a "little world" (I, 11). Although the invasion fails, the tactics of the Martian expeditionary force yet produce the desired effect: "They do not," the narrator comments on his brother's report of the advance on London, "seem to have aimed at extermination so much as at complete demoralisation" (I, 17). In the end, the romance is about demoralization, showing proud Martians dying ignominiously and proud human beings utterly stupefied and humiliated. Even as he writes six years after the event, the narrator still sees humanity in an altered aspect; by night he dreams of London revisited by the plague of black smoke, by day he watches crowds of businessmen and shoppers "haunting the streets that I have seen silent and wretched, going to and fro, phantasms in a dead city, the mockery of life in a galvanised body" (II, 10). And, more ominously, he observes sightseers on Primrose Hill come to gawk at the tripod that still stands there while their children play obliviously in the flower-beds. Human beings resume their lives, as before. The spectators who drank ginger-beer on Horsell Common now rubberneck among the Martian relics in London. History slides toward the museum; horror becomes a tourist attraction. The descendants of the survivors are in peril of losing the indispensable lesson of the Martian invasion announced in the book's first sentence—that "intelligences greater than man's" are "yet as mortal *as his own* [my italics]."

The narrator's brooding, cautionary text exists lest they forget.

B.

That the principal narrator of *The First Men in the Moon*, the fledgling dramatist Bedford, should remain incognito on his return to earth by adopting the alias "Wells"—"a thoroughly respectable sort of name" (ch. 20)—is a measure of how much more whimsical and self-conscious a book this is than *The War of the Worlds*. Later, when the physicist Cavor reports his findings inside the hollow moon, he sheds scientific description for old folklore and jokingly likens the moon's bluish texture to Gruyère cheese. And we are certain that this lunar romance is as full of moonshine as speculation. In the preface to the Atlantic edition, Wells described it as "an imaginative spree" and evaluated it as likely the best of his scientific romances. In fact, *The First Men in the Moon* celebrates the fantastic while the philosophical narrator of the Martian invasion prefers documentary reportage. The voyage through space, the astronauts' weightlessness, the spectacular flowering of the lunar vegetation, the pursuit and flight through the labyrinthine caves beneath the moon, the bellowing of the "gruntulous" mooncalves and the battle in the Selenite slaughterhouse, Bedford's race against time as freezing night overtakes the moon's surface, Cavor's climactic interview with the cystic Grand Lunar himself—all these marvels are presented with a picturesque and confident expansiveness that makes *The First Men in the Moon* the closest thing to a pure flight of fancy among Wells's longer fictions.

Jules Verne was still alive when *The First Men in the Moon* was published in 1901, and his dislike for the book is notorious. His own version of a flight to the moon had been published in 1864, and he took cranky pride in what he considered its authenticity, its fidelity to science. He sniffed at Wells's use of an anti-gravitational material ("Cavorite") as motor force for his vehicle, as opposed to the 900-foot cannon, extrapolated from the gigantic Rodman guns used in the American Civil War, which launches Verne's space capsule in *From the Earth to the Moon*. (In fairness to Wells, it should be observed that he *did* adapt Verne's idea in *The War of the Worlds*, whose Martians were shot to earth out of a "huge gun" [I, 1].) But for all its scientific respectability, *From the Earth to the Moon* is negligible as narrative—an inflated set of lectures on popular science strung onto a tenuous, rarely interesting plot. *The First Men in the Moon* is unabashedly fantastic in content, though characteristically engaging in form and intellectually energetic. Although critics have sometimes found its structure awkward and its ideology confused, its partisans have included the Argentine fantasist Jorge Luis Borges and, more surprisingly, T. S. Eliot who found "quite unforgettable" the lunar sunrise and other emphatically romantic scenes that redeem Wells's work from being gifted "journalism." Rebecca West, recognizing the intricate playfulness of the work, has called *The First Men in the Moon* a "complete Meccano set for the mind." [3] And it is the model for one of the great fantastic voyages of modern literature, C. S. Lewis' *Out of the Silent Planet* (1939).

The First Men in the Moon is gloriously inventive, but it is no idle space opera. Fantasy and satire are integral in the narrative, and this last of Wells's major romances of his early period is his greatest homage to and imitation of *Gulliver's Travels*. Wells sent men to the moon, as he indicated in the 1934 preface to his romances, "in order to look at mankind from a distance." In one explicit way, at least, the lunar satire picks up the thread of speculation where *The War of the Worlds* left off, with the artilleryman comparing the Martians to men and the indigenous earthlings to ants: "It's just men and ants. There's the ants build their cities, live their lives, have wars, revolutions, until the men want them out of the way, and then they go out of the way" (II, 7). In the moon, once Bedford and Cavor arrive, it's also just ants and men, except that the ants don't get out of the way at man's bidding. The civilization of the ant-like Selenites is more advanced than man's, though more chilling and dystopian in its specialization of functions and intellectual topheaviness. The Selenites are too prudent to allow their habitat to be exploited by human adventurers, but the narrative raises once more the questions of colonialism and humanism, as Bedford makes explicit when he drunkenly refers to the moon as "part of the White Man's Burden" (ch. 10).

The Gulliver-figure in all this is Cavor, a scientist quite unlike the psychologically crippled Griffin and the depraved Moreau. Cavor is a moral blank—a short, fat, uncoordinated, absent-minded "marionette" of a man (ch. 1). A technical whiz, he is obtuse about the practical and ethical consequences of his research; until Bedford advises him, he cannot imagine a use for the gravity-nullifying material he has invented other than the pleasure of having it named after himself. Such naiveté is, as

Swift's Gulliver also demonstrates, not simply amusing but willful and dangerous. When his testing of Cavorite causes an industrial accident that damages homes nearby and might have asphyxiated the whole planet, Cavor covers it up to avoid lawsuits: "I cannot possibly pay for the damage I have done, and if the real cause of this is published it will lead only to heart-burning and the obstruction of my work. One cannot foresee everything, you know, and I cannot consent for one moment to add the burden of practical considerations to my theorising" (ch. 2). It is a familiar plea of developers of new and risky technologies.

Deficient in consciousness and conscience, Cavor is easily manipulated by the crassly practical Bedford, who is motivated by the need to evade his creditors and the desire to strike it rich quick on the moon. "He was to make the stuff," Bedford says, cutting through his ignorance of the science underlying Cavor's experiments, "and I was to make the boom" (ch. 1). The upshot is that neither character has a moral imagination. While Bedford has the dramatist's gift for recording the wonder of things unknown and is our access to the romance of the journey, he is morally bankrupt. Cavor the technician provides a crisp, precise sociology of the Selenites in his final radio dispatches, but his imagination is so limited that he can neither perceive his own danger nor effectively evaluate the society he observes.

The human imagination tends to be circumscribed by human experience; we imagine the other not *as other* but in familiar terms. Bedford, for example, finds it nearly impossible to visualize the ant's face under a Selenite helmet: "I think that our incurable anthropomorphism made us imagine there were human heads inside their masks" (ch. 13). Discussing their unanticipated position as the first men *in* the moon, Cavor and Bedford realize that unexamined assumptions kept them from imagining a lunar world different from the earthly model:

> "We never thought of a world inside the moon."
> "No."
> "How could we?"
> "We might have done. Only—one gets into habits of mind" (ch. 12).

The flight to the moon and the experience on it are shock therapy for the deficient imagination. Describing the feeling of weightlessness, Bedford is stymied by the lack of precedents; like the narrator of *The War of the Worlds* trying to describe a Martian, he gropes clumsily for language and for the nearest terrestrial analogues:

> It was the strangest sensation conceivable, floating thus loosely in space, at first indeed horribly strange, and when the horror passed, not disagreeable at all, exceedingly restful! Indeed the nearest thing in earthly experience to it that I know is lying on a very thick soft feather bed. But the quality of utter

detachment and independence! I had not reckoned on anything like this. I had expected a violent jerk at starting, a giddy sense of speed. Instead I felt—as if I were disembodied. It was not like the beginning of a journey; it was like the beginning of a dream (ch. 4).

The famous sixth and seventh chapters, the accounts of the landing on the moon and of the dawn, constitute the most sustained assault on "habits of mind." Anticipating the visual wonders of time-lapse photography and looking back to the animation of the earth as described in Book VII of Milton's *Paradise Lost*, the chapters are a celebration of metamorphosis. As he watches through the concave glass of the spherical spacecraft, Bedford sees the bleak, pale landscape startle into life and color. The activity on the moon's surface is intense and rapid: "quickening," "straining," "thrusting," "bristling," "swelling," "hurrying tumultuously." Bedford feels his imagination liberated and exalted: "It was like a miracle, that growth. So, one must imagine, the trees and plants arose at the Creation, and covered the desolation of the new-made earth" (ch. 7). [4]

The immediate effect of this imaginative regeneration is that Bedford and Cavor lose their inhibitions and turn their lunar landing into a roadside picnic. Leaping and cavorting through the jungle springing up around them, they soon wander so far in the dense vegetation that they lose sight of their sphere. Hunger and thirst weaken them, and they see erect creatures of ant-like form treading through the underbrush. Just before being escorted underground by their captors, these "two poor terrestrial castaways" desperately eat some lunar vegetables; they turn out to be hallucinogens under whose influence Bedford has a brief revelation of Cavor's folly: "It also occurred to me that he erred in imagining that he had discovered the moon—he had not discovered it, he had only reached it" (ch. 10). In their subsequent adventures both men keep falling victim to that delusion: Cavor using pidgin English to try to communicate with the Natives, and Bedford acting like a swashbuckling conquistador punching and slashing his way through the lunar caves and leaving a trail of dead Selenites behind him.

The experience inside the moon affects Cavor more profoundly than it does Bedford. When they finally fight their way out of the cave of the butchers and return to the surface, Bedford is intent on survival, on recovering the spacecraft, flying home to earth, and organizing a return expedition to strip the moon of its mineral wealth. But Cavor has seen enough to know that, as the first ambassadors from earth to the moon, he and Bedford have botched a unique opportunity. He is reluctant to leave and begins to fear that his scientific invention will be misused. "It was I found the way here, but to find a way isn't always to be master of a way" (ch. 17). Looking at the gold Bedford is preparing to carry back to earth, Cavor foresees "governments and powers" scrambling to get a piece of lunar real estate—and they will not even have the Martians' excuse that they needed to find

53

a new habitat to preserve their species.

Cavor himself does not make it back to the sphere with Bedford; he is captured by Selenite pursuers, though he seems almost to desire his return to the moon's interior. [5] Bedford has neither Cavor's self-abnegation nor his conscientious misgivings. Believing Cavor dead, he is simply glad to have made it out alive himself. On the homeward voyage the weightlessness gives Bedford a disturbing (and again momentary) hallucinogenic detachment when he sees himself as a type of human pretension and triviality, "not only as an ass, but as the son of many generations of asses" (ch. 19). But the vision does not pass into analysis.

After he arrives back in England, carelessly loses his Cavorite sphere to Master Tommy Simmons (for whose death he coolly disclaims responsibility), and cashes in his two golden crowbars, Bedford has nothing to show for his experience except the mere fact of survival, and maybe a story he can sell to the magazines. His moral imagination remains hostage to his own self-centered frustrations:

> The net result of the great experiment presented itself as an absolute failure. It was a rout and I was the sole survivor. It was an absolute collapse and this was the final disaster. There was nothing for it but to save myself, and as much as I could in the way of prospects from our *debacle* (ch. 20).

But Bedford's melodrama of absolutes and finalities is premature. He isn't the sole survivor; even as he is writing "The End" to chapter 20 with a confident "flourish" (ch. 21), Cavor is alive and journeying to the center of the moon where the Grand Lunar presides. Weeks later, after his manuscript has begun appearing in magazine installments and while he is putting his life back together in Mediterranean resorts, Bedford gets astounding news. A Dutch researcher working on electromagnetic technology has intercepted radio transmissions from the moon—in English.

The six substantial dispatches that come through from Cavor alter and enlarge the perspectives of Bedford's narrative. He can no longer treat the voyage to the moon merely as melodrama, as a detachable episode in his life. The edited transcripts with commentaries he appends to his manuscript open his narrative to new questions and less comfortable analyses. Cavor's reports come as a jolt to Bedford's imaginative inertia. The glib assurance that life goes on with which he ended chapter 20 and, he thought, closed the book on the Selenites and their world, is no longer tenable. His neat ending grows ragged and inconclusive. And his revised book closes not with a self-satisfied celebration of survival but a darkly comic glimpse into the lunar underworld, a nasty death, and a chilling silence.

Cavor's earliest dispatches are largely topographical and disclose an intricate world of caverns, galleries, and shafts far below the outer shell Bedford had visited. We glimpse lunar cities, wildlife, transportation, and the luminous, milky blue sea at the moon's center. But the essential transmissions are those that describe the social order and Cavor's conversations with the Grand Lunar. His education in the "natural History" of the moon's inhabitants is entrusted to a pair of tutors (and guards) whom Wells whimsically names Phi-oo and Tsi-puff. The lunar society Cavor observes is passionless and hierarchical, with each Selenite "a perfect unit in a world machine" (ch. 23). Laborers whose hands are specially developed live in the outer, "pastoral" regions near the surface; those whose specialties are more intellectual—the administrators, scholars, and technocrats —inhabit the center and have atrophied limbs and enormous heads that leave them so topheavy that they are fragile and almost immobile. "Some of the profounder scholars are altogether too great for locomotion," Cavor writes gullibly, "and are carried from place to place in a kind of sedan tub, wabbling jellies of knowledge that enlist my respectful astonishment" (ch. 23).

Cavor's open-mouthed tour of the inner sanctum of Selenite society has the comic horror of Gulliver's third voyage, particularly Swift's accounts of scientific experimentation in Laputa and the Academy of Lagado. The vocational training of the youths Cavor calls "mooneys" is reported with a furious energy that is Swiftian in its indictment both of misguided Selenite utopianism and of the terrestrial *status quo*:

> I came upon a number of young Selenites, confined in jars from which only the fore-limbs protruded, who were being compressed to become machine-minders of a special sort. The extended 'hand' in this highly developed system of technical education is stimulated by irritants and nourished by injection while the rest of the body is starved. Phi-oo, unless I misunderstood him, explained that in the earlier stages these queer little creatures are apt to display signs of suffering in their various cramped situations, but they easily become indurated to their lot; and he took me on to where a number of flexible-limbed messengers were being drawn out and broken in. It is quite unreasonable, I know, but these glimpses of the educational methods of these beings have affected me disagreeably. I hope, however, that may pass off and I may be able to see more of this aspect of this wonderful social order. That wretched-looking hand sticking out of its jar seemed to appeal for lost possibilities; it haunts me still, although, of course, it is really in the end a far more humane proceeding than our earthly method of leaving children to grow into human beings, and then making machines of them (ch. 23).

The carelessness and shortsightedness that are Cavor's characteristic weaknesses betray him once he achieves the long-sought meeting with the Grand Lunar. Cavor makes a sorry appearance as earthly ambassador, standing unkempt, unshaven, and in tatters in the domed hall of the Grand Lunar. But the moon's ruler is no less absurd, an immense bladder of a brain stretching for many yards over a tiny pair of eyes and a shriveled little body. "It was great. It was pitiful," Cavor remarks (ch. 24). The Grand Lunar, literary descendant of a pair of Swiftian monarchs—the morally earnest King of Brobdingnag and the ineffectual King of Laputa attended by his "flappers"—scrutinizes and interrogates Cavor while flunkies spray his scalp with cooling liquids. While discoursing on human housing, libraries, transport, and weather, Cavor makes the Gulliverian error of discussing terrestrial warfare, the history of human conquest and pillage, and the suspicious fact that he is radioing messages to earth.

The Grand Lunar reflects critically on the "strange superficiality and unreasonableness of [man], who lives on the mere surface of a world, a creature of waves and winds and all the chances of space, who cannot even unite to overcome the beasts that prey upon his kind, and yet who dares to invade another planet" (ch. 24). More practically, the king has grasped that the human route to the moon depends on Cavor—who alone knows the formula for making Cavorite, who may at any time transmit that formula in his dispatches to earth, and who has already given whatever earthlings may be receiving his messages extensive field reports on the lay of the land within the moon. Suddenly, Cavor's messages cease coming, and then Bedford hears "like a cry in the night" a couple of staccato transmissions, fragmentary and desperate communications beginning, "I was mad to let the Grand Lunar know——" (ch. 25).

Commentary is as superfluous at the end of *The First Men in the Moon* as at the end of *Gulliver's Travels*. Quite rightly the narrative simply stops. We know how inadequate both Bedford and Cavor are as moral exemplars or commentators, and in any case the narrative has become too multivalent to be tidily summed up in an epilogue. Instead, the romance ends shockingly with Bedford's vision of Cavor's likely death, the imagined screams, the suffocation, the speechlessness, the isolation. For once, Bedford's penchant for melodrama serves the purpose:

> I see, almost as plainly as though I had seen it in actual fact, a blue-lit dishevelled Cavor struggling in the grip of a great multitude of those insect Selenites, struggling ever more desperately and hopelessly as they swarm upon him, shouting, expostulating, perhaps even at last fighting, and being forced backward step by step out of all speech or sign of his fellows, for evermore into the Unknown—into the dark, into that silence that has no end (ch. 25).

The last two words neatly demolish the earlier "The End" Bedford had planned for chapter 20—and the conclusiveness and finality and human control such endings imply.

NOTES

1. These are not, of course, unfamiliar phenomena. As I am writing, the first nuclear power accident at Three Mile Island in Pennsylvania is several weeks old. While the outcome of the accident was not predictable, the newspaper and television coverage of the danger—done up in journalism's best "live" soap opera fashion—was so predictable that great portions of the public remained inert or found the event entertaining. Already some enterprising concessionaire has marketed a T-shirt inscribed, "I survived TMI (I think)." Wells's portrait of blasé Londoners, rural hucksters and extravagant journalists remains pertinent.

2. The Adamic anti-type in science fiction is traceable to Mary Shelley's futuristic novel about a global plague, *The Last Man* (1826).

3. Americans know Meccano sets as Erector sets.

4. There are verbal as well as pictorial resemblances between chapter 7 and the Miltonic account of the creation of the vegetable kingdom in *Paradise Lost*, VII, 309-328.

5. Cavor's version of this event in ch. 22—a peaceful surrender to the Selenites—contradicts Bedford's story in ch. 18 of a violent ambush.

VI
SHORT FICTION

In his *Experiment in Autobiography* (8:1), Wells deprecates his "single sitting stories" as work "ground out" to subsidize his early career and, in their later reincarnations in anthologies, as unlooked-for insurance against his declining years. In fact, the short fiction includes many sophisticated and powerful tales and two imperfect though fascinating novellas. Apart from its usefulness in turning a quick profit, the short story form furnished Wells a playground of the mind, a small, enclosed space in which he could try out issues and techniques that might be more fully employed in the longer scientific romances. The title of his first volume of stories, *The Stolen Bacillus and Other Incidents*, accurately names the priority of most of the tales; they are basically reports of exhilarating or disturbing incidents, natural or preternatural, fantastic or technological shocks to the accepted norms and givens of daily life. But, as in the longer fictions, a Wellsian incident is seldom treated merely incidentally but as an occasion for speculation and critical inquiry

Perhaps the kind of speculative story most often associated with Wells is the predictive tale like "The Argonauts of the Air" (1895), [1] a forecast of the invention of flying machines—a theme whose implications never ceased to intrigue Wells. (*The War in the Air* most extensively, but also *When the Sleeper Wakes*, *The World Set Free*, and the late utopian future history, *The Shape of Things to Come*, all manifest the continuing Wellsian romance with flight.) Wells himself took a grim satisfaction in his prediction of tank warfare, a dozen years before its actual occurrence during the first World War, in "The Land Ironclads" (1903). Generally, though, despite their interest as illustrations of Wells's technological imagination, the predictive stories are not among his most accomplished fictions. The best of them may be "Filmer" (1901), the biography of the putative inventor of the first workable heavier-than-air flying machine. It focuses not on the fact of mechanical innovation but on its psychological implications for the inventor, who commits suicide on his day of glory. As a tale that speculates about "that recurring wonder of the littleness of the scientific man in the face of the greatness of his science," "Filmer" belongs in the company of those Wellsian fictions that ponder the insecurity of human intelligence and the tentativeness of civilization.

In one of his finest stories, "The Star" (1897), Wells takes the issue of the vulnerability of human civilization to an apocalyptic conclusion. In this panorama of disaster and panic occasioned by the approach of a huge comet to the earth, millions die, the climate grows hot, the planet's surface is remade by earthquakes and tidal waves, the lunar cycle is lengthened to eighty days, and the remnant of the human population migrates to the cool poles. The earth is barely rescued from annihilation by the interposition of the moon between the earth and the onrushing comet. The human species survives, but the tale offers neither reassurance nor the satisfaction of a minimally happy ending. The final paragraph takes us to Mars where astronomers—relatives, presumably, of the unsuccessful adventurers in *The War of the Worlds*—are observing through telescopes the spectacle of the collision of the comet and the moon and are preparing scientific papers on what they take to be the minor damage done to the earth. Wells's narrator then neatly upends homocentrist pretensions: "Which only shows how small the vastest human catastrophes may seem, at a distance of a few million miles."

Wells's perspectives on the contingency of civilization are not always extraterrestrial. "In the Abyss" (1896), a description of a primitive civilization at the bottom of the sea, is challenging and frightening in its suggestion that even on our own planet we may not be alone. Even a lightweight tale like "The Stolen Bacillus" (1894), in spite of its snickering treatment of both biological warfare and the tactics of modern terrorism, demonstrates the perverse human capacity to destroy its own culture. "The Empire of the Ants" (1905), a story with ideological links to *The First Men in the Moon*, ends with a vision of the gradual recolonizing of the earth by a remarkably clever and swiftly breeding strain of ants moving steadily through the Brazilian interior: "By 1920 they will be half-way down the Amazon. I fix 1950 or '60 at the latest for the discovery of Europe." Because we know what ensued from the "discovery" of the Americas by European conquistadors, the closing sentence is ominous. It puts human culture in its place—and that place is not at the center of creation.

Wells inquires more extensively and mythically into the nature of civilization in a pair of novellas published in 1897. "A Story of the Stone Age" and "A Story of the Days to Come" are picaresque fictions, anthologies of episodes from the lives of a paleolithic man and woman and of a couple from twenty-second-century London. The novellas are symmetrical in design and ideologically complementary: in each the protagonists are malcontents, exiled from the dominant culture, whether tribal or industrial; each is a story of fitness and survival; each portrays the hopeful genesis of a new stage in civilization that will replace and transcend a dying culture. Both stories depict individuals tensed against the societies that produced them and both offer a disquieting vision of the price in blood, anguish, and brutalizing labor that is paid for the achievements and adornments of civilization.

In the closing pages of "Days to Come," Wells explicitly connects the story of Ugh-lomi and Eudena, exiles from the tribe of Uya, with the story of Denton and Elizabeth, economic and social rebels in futuristic London; the four misfits all occupy the same physical space, and Denton broods on the future, "trying in obedience to his instinct to find his place and proportion in the scheme" of human and cosmic history, while standing in the very spot that once was "the squatting-place of the children of Uya" (ch. 5). To be civilized in the paleolithic age is nearly to die in the efforts to secure food, to tame a horse, to kill a grizzly bear; to be civilized in the future metropolis is to be born wealthy enough to live in elegant and extravagant indolence while others, unlucky enough to be born without money or to lose their money, labor at the production of luxuries they cannot enjoy. In the Stone Age, the price of civilization, though high in bodily harm, seems justified by the aspirations; in the days to come the price—psychological, spiritual, and physical—seems disproportionate to the purchase.

But Wells's point is not to suggest a mere linear devolution from stone-age vigor to post-modern decadence. The parallel design of the novellas emphasizes the *persistence* of certain human behaviors and cultural patterns. Human history is a story of continuities and recrudescences. Ugh-lomi establishes his independence by beating up his rival, Uya; Denton, thrust from a secure middle-class life into menial work in the Labour Company, quickly learns that in the twenty-second century "the fist ruled...even as it was in the beginning" (ch. 4). Futuristic man discovers how much he remains stone-age man: "After all we are just poor animals, rising out of the brute" (ch. 3). The poignancy of the mock-fairy-tale ending of "The Stone Age" lies in its placement of the provisional success of individual, heroic struggle within a larger, impersonal, Darwinian pattern of struggle: "Thereafter for many moons Ugh-lomi was master and had his will in peace. And on the fulness of time he was killed and eaten even as Uya had been slain" (ch. 5). The same bitter contrast between individual suffering and social progress emerges when the future hero and heroine reflect on the misery of life in the Labour Company. Denton: "It will pass." Elizabeth: "We shall pass first" (ch. 3).

Wells revisited his twenty-second century twice in *When the Sleeper Wakes* and in "A Dream of Armageddon" (1901). The two novellas and the two later works represent a diffuse effort by Wells to work out a comprehensive explanation of human history, a myth which might explain why the distance between stone-age and future man is so slight and why civilization remains both the elusive goal and the nemesis of human activity. As in *The Time Machine*, the cosmos is indifferent to human effort, to the small risings and fallings and recoveries of the species. As Eudena listens rapt to Ugh-lomi narrate his gory murder of Uya, she is observed by silent, stellar witnesses—which also observe Denton and Elizabeth 50,000 fictional years later—which also observe the readers reading those fictions in "real" time. In their constancy and stability, those witnesses mock the splendor of Ugh-lomi and Eudena's small achievements and of ours: "It was a splendid time, and the stars that look down on us looked down on her, our ancestor—who has been dead now these fifty thousand years" (ch. 1).

Both novellas suffer from failures in conception and execution. The language of "The Stone Age" is embarrassingly clumsy and stilted at times, while the plot of "Days to Come" dishonestly resolves Denton and Elizabeth's fall from social favor. Still, these short works are representative of Wells's ambivalence towards civilization in the great decade bounded by *The Time Machine* (1895) and *A Modern Utopia* (1905). "A Story of the Days to Come" is the richer of the two, its world exercised a greater hold on Wells's imagination, and along with *When the Sleeper Wakes*, it has influenced the history of the modern urban dystopia. But in its awkward effort to create an anthropologically authentic portrait of prehistoric humanity, "A Story of the Stone Age" is one of Wells's most daring experiments and his most interesting failure. Despite their deficiencies, the two novellas document the Wellsian notions that human history is but a small part of planetary history and that the story of civilization is itself a short story.

Wells is renowned for perfecting a pseudo-documentary technique in his speculative fictions—what the narrator of the little-known romance *The Sea Lady* calls "the true affidavit style" (4:1). But the mythic novellas are reminders of his imaginative versatility and the breadth of his range. "The Stolen Body" (1898), one of his several exercises in the tale of the preternatural, displays Wells at the height of his powers. A story of body snatchers from a parallel world who are loosed on the primary world by scientific dilettantes toying with mental telepathy, it provokes typical Wellsian questions: What are the consequences of aimless experimentation? In what respects is curiosity contaminated by failures of intelligence or foresight or moral sensibility? Are there limits beyond which human beings trespass only at the peril of life and sanity? Similar questions underlie the preternatural phenomena in stories like "The Flowering of the Strange Orchid" (1894), "The Crystal Egg" (1897), and "The Door in the Wall" (1906), the last of which is probably closer in spirit than anything Wells wrote to the luminous mysticism of George Macdonald's "The Golden Key" (1867) and *Lilith* (1895).

At the other end of Wells's spectrum are the comic stories concerning human manipulation of mysterious events or technological inventions for mundane ends. That group of tales includes "The Purple Pileus" (1896), "The Man Who Could Work Miracles" (1898), and "The Truth About Pyecraft" (1903). One of the funniest stories in this group, "The New Accelerator" (1901), is a prose cartoon about an unscrupulous professor who manufactures a kind of super-amphetamine that speeds up physical movement. Professor Gibberne combines the technical expertise of Cavor with the business sense of Bedford, and the gullible narrator is so impressed by the idea of a miracle drug that he is swept up unquestioningly into the "trip" Gibberne arranges for him. The drug allows the user to make mischief with impunity because he moves so quickly that his victims can't see him and, as he watches the rest of the world go by in slow motion, people appear as mechanisms and caricatures. The psychedelic vision afforded by the drug is inevitably inhumane. Promenaders look like dummies; a wink or a gesture becomes a grotesque thing; a suitor's innocent smile slows to a leer. For all its madcap charm, "The New Accelerator" is as pointed as any of Wells's soberer speculations. The professor and narrator plan to push the sale of the new drug as fast as possible despite any ethical reservations they might have about its use. The only problems they consider themselves competent to address are technical and marketing ones:

> Like all potent preparations it will be liable to abuse. We have, however, discussed this aspect of the question very thoroughly, and we have decided that this is purely a matter of medical jurisprudence and altogether outside our province. We shall manufacture and sell the Accelerator, and, as for the consequences—we shall see.

Several of the best stories are visionary in theme and method. In these tales the protagonists acquire, usually accidentally or involuntarily, some special angle or instrument of vision that enables them to see familiar reality freshly and unfamiliar reality with both wonder and terror. Often these tales are narrated not by the protagonist but by a skeptical rationalist, an outsider describing and assessing mysterious events to which he has been a (generally unwilling) witness. The narrator characteristically tells his story in a state of shell-shock, his comfortable and fundamental presuppositions about how reality works no longer secure.

In two of the visionary tales, "The Remarkable Case of Davidson's Eyes" (1895) and "The Plattner Story" (1896), the transformations of perception occur in laboratories, and the locale dramatizes the upsetting of scientific certitudes and mental habits by a sudden eruption of visionary experience. In Davidson's case a thunderstorm triggers a displacement of vision; while his body and other sensory experience remain rooted in England, visually he exists on a bleak Antarctic island. In "The Plattner Story" a green powder explodes in a school chemistry lab and causes the teacher to disappear for nine days. When Plattner abruptly returns as a literal nine-days' wonder, he tells of a numinous other world lit by a green sun, a limbo inhabited by souls who keep watch over the living in our world. Scientists eager to dismiss Plattner's story as hallucination are stymied by one incontrovertible fact: all his body organs and features have shifted position so that his anatomical structure is a mirror reversal of what it was before he disappeared. The investigators are mortified and disgruntled; although publicly skeptical about his claims, they are in fact embarrassed by the body that exists as a living refutation of scientific assurance and rational sufficiency.

Variants on the visionary mode can be found in "Under the Knife" (1896) in which the narrator, on a hospital operating table, inhales chloroform and goes on a mental journey whose satirical and spiritual texture recalls the conventions of medieval dream-visions. The narrator's dream of himself in the company of a host of "naked intelligences" moving through the cosmos may have given Olaf Stapledon the idea for the pilgrimage of disembodied minds in *Star Maker* (1937). In "The Crystal Egg," another of Wells's Martian satires, a strange crystal allows an unhappy shopkeeper to escape the demands of his domestic life by providing a magic—or electronic—window on the arcadian world of Mars. (When the shopkeeper is startled by an immense pair of eyes peering at him from the other side of the crystal, the reader may be reminded of J. R. R. Tolkien's *palantir* in *The Lord of the Rings* in which the eye of Sauron appears to those seeking a glimpse of the land of Mordor.) Eventually the shopkeeper, a prototype of the television addict, abandons his work so that "he might comfort himself with what was fast becoming the most real thing in his existence." He is later found dead, clutching the crystal. An often anthologized visionary tale, "The Country of the Blind" (1904), is a parable about an El Dorado-like region in the Andes inhabited by blind people and accidentally discovered by a sighted man. While coldly refuting the proverb about the one-eyed man being king among the blind, the tale asserts the necessity of spiritual vision; blindness is treated not as a clinical phenomenon but as a metaphor for atrophied imagination and rigid dogmatism.

In his famous essay "On Fairy Stories" Tolkien argues, "Anyone inheriting the fantastic device of language can say *the green sun*. Many can then imagine or picture it. But that is not enough." We may wonder if Tolkien was dimly remembering Wells's green sun in "The Plattner Story," but whether or not the passage contains an allusion to Wells, it furnishes a hint of the difference between the major author of modern science fiction and the major author of modern fantasy. Tolkien as critic and artist was committed to the "sub-creating" of "Secondary Worlds," discrete worlds of imagination fully realized, independent, and credible on their own terms. By that definition, Wells's visionary stories are not genuine fantasies but engaging speculative exercises. His only fully realized "secondary worlds" are in the utopian romances, *A Modern Utopia* and *Men Like Gods*, books of practical fantasy designed not to create parallel worlds for their own sakes but to provide models for the transformation of the primary world of experience. Even in his most forthrightly fantastic stories, Wells did not subcreate separate worlds but tried to suggest the seamlessness of the realm of experience with the realm of imagination. The narrator of "The Apple" (1896), Wells's fanciful reworking of the temptation of Adam and Eve, suggests the interpenetration of the secondary and primary worlds: "It was as if the real was a mere veil to the fantastic, and here was the fantastic poking through."

Tolkien's imagination envisioned alternative kingdoms of desire, often highly nostalgic, pastoral communities that repudiate industrial technology and question the notions of science and progress; for all their richness of invention of non-human characters and critters, Tolkienian fantasies are essentially conservative and humanist. But for Wells, desirability was in itself never a sufficient recommendation of an alternative; he always greatly admired the anarchist ideal embodied in *News from Nowhere*, but he steadfastly insisted, as in *Men Like Gods* (III,2:4), that Morris' utopia was charmingly irrelevant, "a graceful impossible book." Wells sought to enhance the primary world with humane technology and social planning, to make this world richer, more benign, more fraught with possibility; his vision was utopian where Tolkien's was arcadian; he was as suspicious of Art as Tolkien was of Industry; and he was, under Darwin's and Huxley's tutelage, less convinced than Tolkien that the standard British virtues were necessarily worth preserving.

The distinctively Wellsian quality of Wells's fantastic fiction may be studied in the two final stories to be considered here, both of which are fantastic parables rather than Tolkienian subcreations. In "The Story of the Late Mr. Elvesham" (1896), an old philosopher clings to life by spiking a liqueur with a magic powder which causes him to exchange bodies with the young materialist Mr. Eden. The premise is unblinkingly fantastic, but the heart of the story is the brilliant rendering of the duality of body and personality in the transformed victim. The account of Eden's gradual realization that he has awakened trapped inside the body of Elvesham, that he has in the space of a single night become wrinkled, toothless, thin-voiced, cold-footed, sniffling, bleary-eyed, bony-fingered, loose-skinned, wracked with cough, persistently and disablingly weary and slow while retaining all the desires and sensibilities and the lively consciousness of youth is one of the triumphs of Wells's imagination, the equal of some of the other great metamorphoses in the longer romances. Narrated by Eden "under restraint" in an effort to prove he is not crazy, the tale is closer than any of Wells's to Poe's monologues by demented narrators ("The Black Cat," "Berenice," "The Tell-Tale Heart"). But it is also a typical Wellsian assault on the modern confidence in the explicability of all phenomena and a portrait of a man imprisoned inside a miracle no one can credit. As Eden despairingly comes to see, the explanation of last resort—the explanation modern people apply to make otherwise intractable events tractable—is psychiatric. Unable to persuade anyone of his true identity, he is left with the choice of suicide or the asylum.

"The Man Who Could Work Miracles: A Pantoum in Prose" bypasses the horror of "Elvesham" and combines fantasy with whimsy in the adventures of the garrulous rationalist and materialist, Mr. Fotheringay, who finds himself in astonished possession of miraculous powers of mind over matter. The story follows the brief career of a man of slender intellect gifted with absolute power. Much of that career is devoted to puckish mischief-making, as when Fotheringay irritably tells a constable to go to Hades and immediately finds himself alone. But when he tries to alter nature, his power, neither harnessed by a modest sense of human limits nor wielded with a vigilant presence of mind, becomes cataclysmic. Under the influence of the revivalist Rev. Mr. Maydig, he attempts to duplicate Joshua's feat of making the sun stand still. Phrasing the command in colloquial English and with accurate scientific awareness of which heavenly body is moving, Fotheringay addresses the earth: "Jest stop rotating, will you?" But when the natural rhythms of the planet are interrupted, every person and thing on earth, in obedience to the laws of inertia, is whirled forward into annihilation. In the midst of chaos casually wrought, Fotheringay conceives "a great disgust of miracles" and ends his career with two simultaneous and final wishes: to lose his thaumaturgical powers and to have everything revert to the way it was just before he discovered these powers. Thus the jinni is rebottled, the damage undone, and the story returned full circle (following the form of the "pantoum" of its subtitle) to its opening conversation. As a work of fantasy, this makes a thoroughly absorbing and satisfying retelling of the classic fairy tale of miraculous power, the story of Aladdin from the *Arabian Nights*. And (how Wells would have appreciated this unintended application of his tale!) later readers can hardly help but find in "The Man Who Could Work Miracles" a cautionary fable for the Nuclear Age. [2]

While some of Wells's short fiction was written with the left hand while he worked on the longer romances, the two novellas and a dozen or more short stories belong to his major work. Readers have sometimes overlooked the stories because of the stature of the science-fiction novels and have assumed that the short fiction is inferior. But even many of the flawed tales help reveal the process of Wells's imagination. "The Sea Raiders" (1896), one of his lesser efforts, describes in a crisp you-are-there style the invasion of the English coast by deep-sea monsters; in both substance and method it is a dry run for *The War of the Worlds*. The failure of Fotheringay in handling absolute power is presented with the same mixture of fantasy and farce Wells perfected in the first half of *The Invisible Man*. He published "The New Accelerator" and *The First Men in the Moon* in the same year and they share issues, character types, and techniques; notably, the story anticipates the visual effects of the stop-action or slow-motion camera, as the lunar dawn in the longer work gives a foretaste of time-lapse photography.

But the greatest of Wells's stories do not have to be studied as tailpieces to the novels or patronized as the hackwork of a writer notorious for overproduction. Many can stand on their own as authentic achievements of Wells's resourceful imagination and technical ingenuity. In fact, "A Story of the Days to Come" is in many respects more convincing and coherent than its novelistic sequel, *When the Sleeper Wakes*. The issues of size and scale and of the management of technology Wells raises in "Filmer" are treated more diffusely and with less power in *The Food of the Gods*. *In the Days of the Comet* is a bloated version of "The Star" and of interest chiefly in those passages that imitate the panoramic techniques of the earlier story. And "The Door in the Wall" makes poignant and real the perilous lure of imagination treated so ludicrously in *The Sea Lady*.

Wells's self-criticism in the opening pages of his *Autobiography* is notable for its candor and scrupulousness: "It scarcely needs criticism to bring home to me that much of my work has been slovenly, haggard, and irritated, most of it hurried and inadequately revised" (1:1). But the honest reader and critic will not simply take Wells at his word. His enduring work is the gift of a generous imagination, an exacting but evocative use of language, and passionate intellectual integrity. Wells's short stories and the great romances of 1895-1901 are a testament to both the excellence and the pertinence of science fiction as a literary form; they remain a repository of the exhilaration, reflection, and admonition that are the distinctive aesthetic and moral values of science fiction.

NOTES

1. Tales are dated in this chapter by their initial magazine publication; the dates of Wells's collections of short fiction are given in Section I, C of the Primary Materials at the back of this *Guide*.

2. Wells's intentional prophecy of atomic warfare in *The World Set Free* in this instance reduces the risk in the questionable procedure of attributing unintended meanings to texts.

VII
BIBLIOGRAPHY

What follows in Part I ("Primary Materials") is a description of the most useful avenues into H. G. Wells's own writings. Section A directs the reader to several bibliographies of Wells's works; section B describes the best and the most readily available editions and reprintings of the works; section C is an alphabetical listing of Wells's important works of science fiction and fantasy, including collections of short stories, with thumbnail descriptions of the longer works; section D is a briefer annotated list of some non-fictional works by Wells that have a bearing on his science fiction.

Part II ("Secondary Materials") is a selective bibliography of works about Wells. Wells differs from many other writers studied in the Starmont series in that a vast body of criticism of his work exists—and continues to grow. The secondary bibliography in this *Guide* is limited to important book-length studies or collections of articles on Wells. Section A of Part II discusses bibliographical resources for locating studies of Wells; section B lists the major biographies; section C describes critical books and collections of articles about Wells; section D is an unannotated list of general studies of science fiction in which Wells is prominent or which help establish the historical or generic context in which Wells wrote.

I. PRIMARY MATERIALS

A. BIBLIOGRAPHIES

1. Wells, Geoffrey H. *The Works of H. G. Wells, 1887-1925.* London: Routledge, 1926. The standard bibliography of Wells's writings (excluding the last twenty years of his career).

2. The H. G. Wells Society. *H. G. Wells: A Comprehensive Bibliography.* 3rd edition. London: H. G. Wells Society, 1972. A primary bibliography of all Wells's works and a list of book-length secondary studies.

3. Hammond, J. R. *Herbert George Wells: An Annotated Bibliography of His Works.* New York and London: Garland, 1977. A comprehensive updating of H. G. Wells's work (A, 1 above) with descriptions.

4. Mullen, R. D. "An Annotated Survey of Books and Pamphlets by H. G. Wells." In *H. G. Wells and Modern Science Fiction.* Ed. Darko Suvin and Robert M. Philmus. Lewisburg, PA: Bucknell University Press, 1977, pp. 223-268. An informative review of Wells's entire literary canon, accompanied by an excellent brief bibliographical essay.

5. Hughes, David Y., and Robert M. Philmus. "A Selective Bibliography (with Abstracts) of H. G. Wells's Science Journalism, 1887-1901." In Suvin and Philmus (see no. 4 above), pp. 191-222. A guide to the magazine articles and reviews by Wells in his early years.

B. EDITIONS, COLLECTIONS, REPRINTS

While there are numerous paperback reprints of Wells's early fiction, their accuracy and reliability vary widely. The student seeking the best texts of Wells's work should consult numbers 1, 2, and 3 below. The best texts are, however, often available only in substantial research libraries, and items 4 and 5 list accessible and relatively inexpensive collections of Wells's best-known work. Items 6 and 7 are particularly valuable collections of non-fiction.

1. *The Works of H. G. Wells: Atlantic Edition.* 28 Vols. London and New York: T. Fisher Unwin, 1924-1927. Contains only works originally published before 1924, with new prefaces by Wells. The indispensable edition of his writings, its chief omission for those interested in science fiction is the original *When the Sleeper Wakes* (1899) for which Wells substituted his 1910 revision, *The Sleeper Awakes.*

2. *The Short Stories of H. G. Wells.* London: Ernest Benn, 1927. While the Atlantic edition contains much of the best short fiction, this is a fuller collection.

3. *Seven Famous Novels by H. G. Wells.* New York: Knopf, 1934. A reprinting of the most popular romances written between 1895 and 1906; the texts are not as reliable as those in the Atlantic edition, but the new preface has special relevance to Wells's theory of the scientific romance.

4. Dover Publications reprints:

    a. *Seven Science Fiction Novels of H. G. Wells.* All the major romances of 1895-1906 except *The Sleeper.*

    b. *Three Prophetic Science Fiction Stories of H. G. Wells.* Contains original version of *When the Sleeper Wakes,* "A Story of the Days to Come," and a text of *The Time Machine* that includes an episode in the far future that appeared in a magazine version but was eliminated by Wells from all book editions.

c. *28 Science Fiction Stories of H. G. Wells.* Full texts of *Men Like Gods* and *Star Begotten*, the novellas "A Story of the Stone Age" and "A Story of the Days to Come," and most of the best short stories.

5. *A Modern Utopia.* Ed. Mark R. Hillegas. Lincoln: University of Nebraska Press, 1967. A facsimile of the 1905 edition with a good introduction by the editor; the most accessible text of Wells's fullest utopia.

6. *H. G. Wells: Early Writings in Science and Science Fiction.* Ed. Robert Philmus and David Y. Hughes. Berkeley: University of California Press, 1975. A rich sampling of Wells's literary apprenticeship, with valuable commentaries and explanatory notes by the editors.

7. *H. G. Wells's Literary Criticism.* Ed. Patrick Parrinder and Robert Philmus. Sussex: Harvester; Totowa, NJ: Barnes and Noble, 1980. A valuable selection of prefaces, reviews, and essays ranging from his journalism of 1895 to a 1938 radio broadcast on science fiction.

8. A complete edition of Wells's letters does not exist. The University of Illinois has published several volumes of correspondence between Wells and other writers, of which the most important is: *Henry James and H. G. Wells.* Ed. Leon Edel and Gordon N. Ray. Urbana: University of Illinois Press, 1958. Another useful set of letters is "The Correspondence of Olaf Stapledon and H. G. Wells, 1931-1942." Ed. Robert Crossley in *Science Fiction Dialogues.* Ed. Gary Wolfe. Chicago: Academy Chicago, 1982. The introduction and notes were altered without Crossley's knowledge or consent and include many errors; the texts of the letters are generally printed correctly, but all the other apparatus must be considered unreliable.

C. FICTION

1. *The Country of the Blind and Other Stories.* London: Thomas Nelson and Sons, 1911. A selection of short fiction, mostly previously collected, including five anthologized for the first time:

> "The Beautiful Suit"; "The Country of the Blind"; "The Door in the Wall"; "The Empire of the Ants"; "A Vision of Judgment"

2. *The First Men in the Moon.* London: George Newnes, 1901. Satiric travelogue of human intruders on and in the moon.

3. *The Food of the Gods and How It Came to Earth.* London: Macmillan, 1904. Scientific experiment produces a race of giants.

4. *In the Days of the Comet.* London: Macmillan, 1906. Earth transformed into a social and sexual utopia by vapors of a passing comet.

5. *The Invisible Man: A Grotesque Romance.* London: C. Arthur Pearson, 1897. Social comedy and horror occasioned by a researcher's experiments on himself.

6. *The Island of Dr. Moreau.* London: William Heinemann, 1896. Parable of creation, with exiled surgeon attempting to impose humanity on animals.

7. *Men Like Gods.* London, New York, Toronto, Melbourne: Cassell, 1923. Twentieth-century British tourists find themselves in a parallel universe with an achieved utopia.

8. *A Modern Utopia.* London: Chapman & Hall, 1905. Part narrative, part philosophical argument, Wells's fullest blueprint for a utopian civilization.

9. *The Plattner Story and Others.* London: Methuen, 1897. About half the stories in Wells's second anthology are science fiction:

> "The Apple," "The Argonauts of the Air," "A Catastrophe," "The Cone," "In the Abyss," "In the Modern Vein: An Unsympathetic Love Story," "The Jilting of Jane," "The Lost Inheritance," "The Plattner Story," "Pollock and the Porroh Man," "The Purple Pileus," "The Red Room," "The Sad Story of a Dramatic Critic," "The Sea Raiders," "A Slip Under the Microscope," "The Story of the Late Mr. Elvesham," and "Under the Knife."

10. *The Sea Lady: A Tissue of Moonshine.* London: Methuen, 1902. Fantasy about a mermaid in upper middle-class British society; the subtitle says it all.

11. *The Shape of Things to Come: The Ultimate Revolution.* London: Hutchinson, 1933. History of 20th and 21st centuries, leading to utopia; basis of a famous film, *Things to Come*, 1936.

12. *The Sleeper Awakes.* London: Thomas Nelson, 1910. Revision of *When the Sleeper Wakes* (see below), not generally regarded as an improvement, despite the flaws of the original version.

13. *Star Begotten: A Biological Fantasia.* London: Chatto & Windus, 1937. The end of humanity and the birth of star-men ("homo sideralis").

14. *The Stolen Bacillus and Other Incidents.* London: Methuen, 1895. Wells's first anthology of short fiction:

> "Aepyornis Island," "A Deal in Ostriches," "The Diamond Maker," "The Flowering of the Strange Orchid," "The Flying Man," "The Hammerpond Park Burglary," "In the Avu Observatory," "The Lord of the Dynamos," "The Moth," "The Remarkable Case of Davidson's Eyes," "The Stolen Bacillus," "The Temptation of Harringay," "Through a Window," "The Treasure in the Forest," and "The Triumphs of a Taxidermist."

15. *Tales of Space and Time.* London and New York: Harper and Brothers, 1899 [issued 1898]. Two novellas and three of the best short stories:

> "A Story of the Stone Age," "A Story of the Days to Come," "The Star," "The Crystal Egg," and "The Man Who Could Work Miracles."

16. *The Time Machine: An Invention.* New York: Henry Holt; London: Heinemann, 1895. Travel into the far future of our planet, glimpsed from political, biological, cosmic perspectives.

17. *Twelve Stories and a Dream.* London: Macmillan; New York: Macmillan, 1903. Wells's last substantial anthology of new short fiction:

> "A Dream of Armageddon," "Filmer," "The Inexperienced Ghost," "Jimmy Goggles the God," "The Magic Shop," "Miss Winchelsea's Heart," "Mr. Brisher's Treasure," "Mr. Ledbetter's Vacation," "Mr. Skelmersdale in Fairyland," "The New Accelerator," "The Stolen Body," "The Truth About Pyecraft," and "The Valley of Spiders."

18. *The War in the Air, and Particularly How Mr. Bert Smallways Fared While It Lasted.* London: George Bell, 1908. Global war, including bombing of the world's major cities by huge blimps, as witnessed by an English workingman haplessly caught up in events.

19. *The War of the Worlds.* London: William Heinemann, 1898. The Martian invasion of the earth and its consequence.

20. *When the Sleeper Wakes.* London and New York: Harper & Brothers, 1899. Life in an urban megalopolis of the 22nd century under a military dictatorship (see *The Sleeper Awakes* above).

21. *The Wonderful Visit.* London: J. M. Dent; New York: Macmillan, 1895. Mildly satirical fantasy about an angel who visits a small English village.

22. *The World Set Free: A Story of Mankind.* London: Macmillan,

1914. Prophetic fantasy about the achievement of global utopia in the aftermath of nuclear war.

D. NON-FICTION

1. *Anticipations of the Reaction of Mechanical and Scientific Progress upon Human Life and Thought.* London: Chapman & Hall, 1901. Essays attempting to forestall future shock and to predict developments in transportation, class structure, architecture, diplomacy, and other features of modern life. The prime example of Wells as social prophet, *Anticipations* explores issues dramatized in such fiction as *When the Sleeper Wakes*, *The Food of the Gods*, and *A Modern Utopia.* Wells called this collection "the keystone to the main arch of my work."

2. *Experiment in Autobiography: Discoveries and Conclusions of a Very Ordinary Brain (since 1866).* 2 vols. London: Victor Gollancz, 1934. Avoiding a sensational account of his private life, Wells reconstructs his intellectual history and development as a writer, thinker, and social reformer. A thoughtful, fascinating exercise in the art of self-study and a valuable (though not infallible) companion to his fiction.

3. *Mind at the End of its Tether.* London and Toronto: William Heinemann, 1945. Wells's last published work, a strident, despairing pamphlet described in John Brunner's novel *Stand on Zanzibar* as "that grim epitaph for human aspiration."

4. *The Outline of History: Being a Plain History of Life and Mankind.* London: George Newnes, 1920. The best-selling book that revolutionized the teaching and writing of history and made Wells's name a household word in middle-class families; it reaches back to his intellectual roots in the satirists and historians of the eighteenth century and in the evolutionary theories of the nineteenth and forward to his own preoccupation with a utopian future.

5. *H. G. Wells In Love: Postscript to An Experiment in Autobiography*, ed. G. P. Wells. Boston: Little, Brown, 1984. Printed from manuscripts edited by the author's son, this memoir of his extra-marital affairs was not publishable during Wells's lifetime.

II. SECONDARY MATERIALS

A. There is not a good, up-to-date bibliography of books and articles about Wells. The *Comprehensive Bibliography* of the Wells Society (cited in I, A, 2 above) lists books only. Northern Illinois University Press plans a volume on Wells for its series of secondary bibliographies on English authors of the period 1880-1920. Recent work on Wells is regularly announced and reviewed in the British journal, *The Wellsian*, the official publication of the H. G. Wells Society.

B. BIOGRAPHICAL STUDIES

1. Mackenzie, Norman and Jeanne. *The Time Traveller: The Life of H. G. Wells.* London: Weidenfeld & Nicolson, 1973. Published in U.S. as *H. G. Wells: A Biography.* New York: Simon & Schuster, 1973. The most authoritative and complete of several recent biographies of Wells, it makes use of unpublished materials in the H. G. Wells archive at the University of Illinois.

2. West, Anthony. *H. G. Wells: Aspects of a Life.* New York: Random House, 1984. As the subtitle suggests, this biography, by the son of Wells and Rebecca West, aims at interpreting persistent themes in Wells's life. The value of the personal knowledge West brings to his subject is somewhat undercut by his evident biases against his mother.

3. West, Geoffrey. *H. G. Wells.* New York: Norton, 1930. With a preface by H. G. Wells. The first biography written with Wells's cooperation, is necessarily partial; somewhat overshadowed by Wells's own *Experiment in Autobiography*, published four years later.

C. CRITICAL STUDIES

1. Bergonzi, Bernard. *The Early H. G. Wells; A Study of the Scientific Romances.* Manchester: Manchester University Press, 1961. The first major, extended literary interpretation of Wells's science fiction. Emphasizes Wells as world-weary ironist and hence more receptive to the earliest works than to the more polemical post-1899 novels.

2. _____, ed. *H. G. Wells: A Collection of Critical Essays.* Englewood Cliffs, NJ: Prentice-Hall, 1976. Half the

essays deal with the science fiction and several important studies are reprinted, notably those by Robert Philmus, V. S. Pritchett, Robert P. Weeks, Anthony West.

3. Cantrill, Hadley. *The Invasion from Mars*. Princeton: Princeton Univ. Press, 1940. A sociological and psychological study of the effects of Orson Welles' radio broadcast of *The War of the Worlds*; includes a text of the Orson Welles version.

4. Haynes, Roslynn D. *H. G. Wells: Discoverer of the Future*. New York and London: New York Univ. Press, 1980. A study of Wells's scientific education and the impact of science on his literary art.

5. Hillegas, Mark R. *The Future as Nightmare: H. G. Wells and the Anti-Utopians*. New York: Oxford Univ. Press, 1967. The most sustained effort to describe a Wellsian tradition in fiction. Surveys most of the early science fiction, but gives prominence to utopian contexts of *The Sleeper*, *Modern Utopia*, *Men Like Gods*.

6. Huntington, John. *The Logic of Fantasy: H. G. Wells and Science Fiction*. New York: Columbia Univ. Press, 1982. An important new approach to the intellectual structures and rhetorical tactics in the major works.

7. Kagarlitski, J. *The Life and Thought of H. G. Wells*, tr. Moura Budberg. London: Sidgwick and Jackson, 1966. A major Soviet appreciation of Wells. The literary analyses are thoughtful and perceptive; the judgments are frankly Marxist. A very valuable comparative assessment of Wells and Verne.

8. McConnell, Frank. *The Science Fiction of H. G. Wells*. New York: Oxford Univ. Press, 1980. An excellent introduction to Wells, broad in scope, detailed, readable.

9. Nicholson, Norman. *H. G. Wells*. London: Arthur Barker, 1950. An early general study that deserves to be better known. Two chapters on the scientific romances are engagingly written, full of prickly but astute judgments of Wells's successes and failures.

10. Parrinder, Patrick. *H. G. Wells*. New York: Putnam, 1977. Compact, lucid, rewarding study of the whole career. The first three chapters belong to the best literary criticism available on the early Wells.

11. _____, ed. *H. G. Wells: The Critical Heritage*. London and Boston: Routledge and Kegan Paul, 1972. A collection of documents (reviews, letters, diary entries, obituaries) which record the public reception of Wells's work from 1895 to his death. Immensely useful, with both anonymous commentaries and

observations by such writers as Conrad, Verne, Chesterton, Zamyatin, T. S. Eliot, Borges.

12. Philmus, Robert M. *Into the Unknown: The Evolution of Science Fiction from Francis Godwin to H. G. Wells.* Berkeley and Los Angeles: Univ. of California Press, 1970. Each chapter, organized around a theme or issue in early science fiction, studies one of Wells's romances in relation to its predecessors. Rich, learned, but densely written.

13. Raknem, Ingvald. *H. G. Wells and His Critics.* Oslo and London: Allen and Unwin, 1962. A rambling, eccentrically organized study of Wells's sources and influences along with an account of critical reactions to his books. Hard to use; no index.

14. Suvin, Darko and Robert M. Philmus, eds. *H. G. Wells and Modern Science Fiction.* Lewisburg, PA: Bucknell Univ. Press, 1977. The best collection of essays on Wells's science fiction; especially useful are Suvin's introduction, comparative essays on Wells and Zamyatin by P. Parrinder and on Wells and Borges by Philmus, studies on the biological ideas in the fiction by D. Hughes and J. Vernier, and bibliographical essays by R. Mullen and by Philmus and Hughes.

15. Wagar, W. Warren. *H. G. Wells and the World State.* New Haven: Yale Univ. Press, 1961. A penetrating study of the utopian Wells. The essential book for understanding Wells's politics and for assessing the relation of his art to propaganda, especially in the often-ignored later writings.

16. Williamson, Jack. *H. G. Wells: Critic of Progress.* Baltimore: Mirage Press, 1973. An earnest analysis of the conservative and critical force of Wells's fiction; stresses Wells as public educator and as heir of Swift.

D. GENERAL STUDIES AND HISTORIES OF SCIENCE FICTION

1. Aldiss, Brian. *Billion Year Spree: The True History of Science Fiction.* Garden City, NY: Doubleday, 1973.

2. Amis, Kingsley. *New Maps of Hell: A Survey of Science Fiction.* New York: Harcourt Brace, 1960.

3. Clarke, I. F. *The Pattern of Expectation 1664-2001.* New York: Basic Books, 1979.

4. Nicolson, Marjorie Hope. *Voyages to the Moon.* New York: Macmillan, 1948.

5. Parrinder, Patrick. *Science Fiction: Its Criticism and*

Teaching. London and New York: Methuen, 1980.

6. Rose, Mark. *Alien Encounters: Anatomy of Science Fiction.* Cambridge, MA: Harvard Univ. Press, 1981.

7. Scholes, Robert and Eric Rabkin. *Science Fiction: History, Science, Vision.* New York: Oxford Univ. Press, 1977.

8. *Science-Fiction Studies.* Two special issues of the major North American scholarly journal on science fiction: "Science Fiction Before Wells," Vol. 3 (Nov., 1976) and "Science Fiction Through Wells," Vol. 8 (March, 1981).

9. Suvin, Darko. *Metamorphoses of Science Fiction.* New Haven and London: Yale Univ. Press, 1979.

INDEX

Arabian Nights, 20-21, 65
Arnold, Matthew, 13, 20
Ballard, J. G., 16
Belloc, Hilaire, 16
Bellow, Saul, 15
Bible, 28, 33-34, 38, 48
Borges, Jorge Luis, 51
Brunner, John, 16
Butler, Octavia E., 21
Capote, Truman, 17
Clarke, Arthur C., 16
Conrad, Joseph, 41
Darwin, Charles, 9-10, 13, 18, 24, 26, 34, 48, 60, 64
Disney, Walt, 14
Doyle, Sir Arthur Conan, 15
Eliot, T. S., 28, 51
Gibbon, Edward, 20
Huxley, Aldous, 16
Huxley, Thomas H., 12-13, 18, 20, 34, 64
James, Henry, 16-17
Johnson, Samuel, 12, 16, 27
Joyce, James, 17
Kepler, Johannes, 43
Le Guin, Ursula K., 15
Lem, Stanislaw, 21
Lewis, C. S., 15-16, 21, 51
MacDonald, George, 61
Mailer, Norman, 17
Marx, Karl, 9-10
Menzies, William Cameron, 14-15
Milton, John, 53, 57
Moorcock, Michael, 15
Morris, William, 10, 64
Orwell, George, 16
Paine, Thomas, 12
Piercy, Marge, 21
Plato, 12, 16, 20
Poe, Edgar Allan, 17, 64
Shelley, Mary, 14, 34, 57
Singer, Peter, 41
Stapledon, Olaf, 15, 44, 63
Swift, Jonathan, 12, 16, 18, 20, 32, 51-52, 55-56
Tolkien, J. R. R., 63-64
Verne, Jules, 14-15, 50-51

Victoria, Queen, 20
Voltaire, 12
Welles, Orson, 44
Wells, H. G.
  "The Apple," 63
  "The Argonauts of the Air," 58
  "The Crystal Egg," 61, 63
  "The Country of the Blind," 63
  "The Door in the Wall," 61, 66
  "A Dream of Armageddon," 60
  "The Empire of the Ants," 59
  Experiment in Autobiography, 9, 58, 66
  "Filmer," 58, 65
  The First Men in the Moon, 22, 41, 43, 50-56, 59, 65
  "The Flowering of the Strange Orchid," 61
  The Food of the Gods, 11, 15-16, 42, 65-66
  "Human Evolution, an Artificial Process," 41
  "In the Abyss," 59
  In the Days of the Comet, 13, 16, 42-43, 66
  The Invisible Man, 11-12, 30, 36-41, 65
  The Island of Dr. Moreau, 11, 13, 30-36, 40-41
  Kipps, 11
  "The Land Ironclads," 58
  "The Man Who Could Work Miracles," 15, 61, 64-65
  The Man Who Could Work Miracles, 15
  Men Like Gods, 9, 13, 63-64
  Mind at the end of Its Tether, 11
  A Modern Utopia, 10, 13, 29, 35, 61, 63
  "The New Accelerator," 61-62, 65
  "The Plattner Story," 17, 62-63
  "The Province of Pain," 41
  "The Purple Pileus," 61
  "The Remarkable Case of Davidson's Eyes," 62
  The Sea Lady, 61, 66
  "The Sea Raiders," 65
  The Shape of Things to Come, 10, 13, 58
  "The Star," 58-59, 66
  Star Begotten, 11-15, 23
  "The Stolen Bacillus," 58-59
  "The Stolen Body," 61
  "A Story of the Days to Come," 59-61, 65
  "The Story of the Late Mr. Elvesham," 41, 64
  "A Story of the Stone Age," 21, 26, 59-61
  Things to Come, 14-15
  The Time Machine, 11, 13, 20-29, 60-61
  Tono-Bungay, 11
  "The Truth About Pyecraft," 61
  "Under the Knife," 63
  The War in the Air, 13-14, 23, 43, 58
  The War of the Worlds, 11-12, 15, 17-18, 23, 43-52, 59, 65
  When the Sleeper Wakes, 11, 15-16, 26, 58, 60-61, 65
  The World Set Free, 11, 23, 43, 58, 66

Wells, Joseph, 12
Wells, Sarah, 12
West, Geoffrey, 10
West, Rebecca, 51
Whale, James, 14
Wordsworth, William, 22, 29
Zamyatin, Yevgeny, 15

www.ingramcontent.com/pod-product-compliance
Lightning Source LLC
LaVergne TN
LVHW041635070426
835507LV00008B/644